Out of the Earth

Cataloging–in–Publication Data

Romaniello, Kerry Downey
Out of the Earth: A Heritage Farm Coast Cookbook
144 pp., illus., 27 cm

1. Cookery—New England. 2. Farms—New England.
3. Cookery—American. 4. Farms—New England—Pictorial Works.
5. History—New England—Farms.

I. Romaniello, Kerry Downey II. Title
Library of Congress Catalogue Number: 98-61428

ISBN: 0932027-407

Printed in the United States of America
Spinner Publications, Inc., New Bedford, MA 02740

Photography, Design and Cover: John K. Robson & Joseph D. Thomas
Text Editing: Marsha L. McCabe   Image Editing: Jay Avila

Out of the Earth

A Heritage Farm Coast Cookbook

BY

KERRY DOWNEY ROMANIELLO

PHOTOGRAPHY AND DESIGN

John K. Robson & Joseph D. Thomas

Spinner Publications, Inc.

New Bedford, Massachusetts

Primary Supporters

Back Eddy Restaurant
Moby Dick Wharf, Westport, MA

Chefs Collaborative 2000
25 First Street, Cambridge, MA

Coastal Growers Association
61 Hixbridge Road, Westport, MA

Decas Cranberry Company
219 Main Street, Wareham, MA

Massachusetts Cultural Council

Massachusetts Department of Agriculture

Mustard Seed Foundation

Westport Rivers Vineyard & Winery
417 Hixbridge Road, Westport, MA

Sponsors

Apponagansett Bay Vineyard
205 Bakerville Road, S. Dartmouth, MA

John George Farms
291 Slocum Road, N. Dartmouth, MA

Lees Super Market
796 Main Road, Westport, MA

Bittersweet Farm
438 Main Road, Westport, MA

Cardoza's Wine & Spirits
6 Sconticut Neck Road, Fairhaven, MA

Ferolbink Farm
993 Neck Road, Tiverton, RI

Gooseberry Farms
1154 Main Road, Westport, MA

Great Hill Dairy, Inc.
160 Delano Road, Marion, MA

LaFrance Hospitality Co. / White's of Westport
66 State Road, Westport, MA

M & C Restaurant
436 Belleville Avenue, New Bedford, MA

Quansett Nurseries
794 Horseneck Road, S. Dartmouth, MA

Sakonnet Vineyards
162 West Main Road, Little Compton, RI

Spring Valley Water Co.
1941 G.A.R. Highway, Swansea, MA

Credits

Text & Editing

Masha L. McCabe
Robert James Russell, II

Copy Editing

Ruth J. Caswell
Tracy A. Furtado
Robert McCabe
Dianne Wood
Jason Paiva
John-Paul Patricio
Carol Russell

Fund Raising

Hilare A. Downey
Milton P. George
Gay Gillespie
Kerry Downey Romaniello
Robert J. Russell, II

Interviews

Peter Bonome
Paul Costa
Fred Dabney
John Decas
John George Jr.
Howard Gifford
Theresa F. Macomber Gifford
Joetta Kirk
Tim McTague
Peter Peckham
Marie Pray
Richard Pray
Carol Russell
Robert James Russell, III
George Smith
Sue Smith
Eva Sommaripa
Diane Ventura
Ernie Ventura
Ann Ward
Jim Ward
David Wilson

Photography, Design & Illustration

John K. Robson
Joseph D. Thomas
Betse V. Downey
Nina Downey Levesque
Jay Avila

Recipes

Cabot Creamery
Coastal Growers Association
Paul Costa
John DeSouza
Betse V. Downey
Hilare A. Downey
Michael Frady
John George, Jr.
Gray's Grist Mill
Ken Haedrich
Gregory J. Jasinski, Jr.
Albert Lees, III
Donna Macomber
Mike Melo
Paradise Meadow Cranberries
Tim Partridge
Tom Porter
Marie Pray
Timothy Quinn
Agustin Ramos
Judy Rebello
Shirley Mae Robbins
Kerry Downey Romaniello
Paul M. Romaniello
Ronald Romaniello
Lois H. Simon
Sue Smith
Eva Sommaripa
Ana Sortun
Paul Sussman
Ann Ward
Susan Kavanaugh White
Stephen Worden

Acknowledgments

The purpose of this section is to give recognition to the source of an inspiration. As inspiration means God breathed, I thank the Father, the Son and the Spirit, from whom all good things come.

In order of appearance, my sincere and lasting gratitude to:

John and Betse Downey who love and support us all without measure, and encourage us to follow our dreams.

Timothy Downey whose words and presence speak to me almost daily, and every member of my family, immediate and extended, because they make me want to learn, love and be more.

My husband Paul who believes I can do anything, especially be a good mother to Alex and Michael.

Bob and Carol Russell, who welcomed me into their business and into this project. Rob and Bill Russell and their families whose lives give.

All at Coastal Growers Association who show us that when united we will stand. And, also for initiating this project.

The members of the local chapters of Chefs Collaborative 2000 for their commitment to sustainability in word, but more importantly, in action.

Everyone at Spinner for everything.

Hilare Downey (and the board) of the Heritage Farm Coast Trust for the same idea the same day…and SAVE OUR FARMS.

To all the growers, chefs and home cooks who shared their time, their insights, their honesty and their recipes.

John Robson, Joe Thomas and Betse Downey—the photographs paint innumerable words about our beautiful area.

Irene Winkler, Coordinator, and her colleagues at the Pilgrim Resource Conservation and Development District and Southeastern Massachusetts Agricultural Partnership.

Gay Gillespie of the Westport River Watershed Alliance for all her support and help.

The Heritage Coast Farm Project is the result of the collective energies of the Coastal Growers Associations, the Chefs Collaborative 2000, the Heritage Farm Coast Trust, the Westport Rivers Vineyard and Winery, and Spinner Publications, Inc.

Table of Recipes

Contents

CARVER

PLYMOUTH

The Heritage Farm Coast of
southeastern New England
includes southern portions
of Bristol and Plymouth
counties along Buzzards
Bay in Massachusetts, and
the Sakonnet Bay region of
southeastern Rhode
Island. 1881 Atlas of the
City of New Bedford.

So. Carver

ock

Middleboro

W. Wareham

WAREHAM

West S.

North S.

S. Wareham

E.
Wareham

Cohasset
Narrows

Monument

Spring
Hill

East S.

ESTER

Monument
Beach

B
A
R
N

SANDWICH

MARION

Pocasset

S. Sandwich

S

Marsh
Mill

MATTAPOISETT

North F.

Hatchville

MASHPEE

Cotuit

FALMOUTH

N

West F.

East F.

Waquoit

BUZZARDS BAY

Falmouth

Quisset

Woods Holl

GNOLD

Vineyard Haven

Vineyard Grove

Cottage City

COTTAGE
CITY

PASQUE

North Tisbury

MTHA'S VINEYARD

G

TISBURY

EDGARTON

Introduction

He causes grass to grow for the cattle, and vegetation for the service of man, that he may bring forth food out of the earth. — Psalm 104:14

*W*elcome to the Heritage Farm Coast of southeastern New England. This bountiful piece of land stretches languidly along the south coast of Massachusetts into southern Rhode Island, and farm and sea come together in a landscape painter's dream. Here, farmers and fishermen have ploughed earth and sea since colonial times, often within view of each other. This tradition is alive and well today. *Out of the Earth* is the first in a series of three Heritage Farm Coast cookbooks featuring recipes from the region. *From the Sea* and *In the Neighborhood* will follow.

Digging potatoes on the Antone George Farm, Dartmouth, 1934. John Sylvia is walking, Manny Mathews is on the digger.

Courtesy of John George, Jr.

In these pages, you will meet some enterprising people in our agricultural community and explore their farms, gardens and vineyards. You will see that the connection between farmer, seller, buyer, chef and eater is inextricably linked. We hope the recipes, some offered by the author, others from professional chefs and home cooks, will encourage you to enjoy the abundance of this region as well as put a face and name on the produce you buy and prepare.

The birth of New England begins here in our region. Though much has been written about the early settlers, one important aspect of that history has generally been under-stated—food history. A wonderful new culinary culture grew out of the interaction between the settlers and the Native Americans, a flavorful heritage that lives with us today and forms the heart of this book.

A century before the first Thanksgiving and the ensuing devastation wrought by King Philip's War, European explorers cruised the coastline of this new land and often connected peacefully with the native people. The visitors marveled at the beauty and abundance of land and water, and powerful exchanges of ideas and information took place. By the early 1600s, the time had come for the interlopers to become residents.

The Puritans, and later the Quakers, left Great Britain in pursuit of religious freedom (though, ironically, the Puritans were not tolerant of Quaker beliefs). The two groups arrived with a variety of backgrounds in agriculture, commerce, education and religion, each enterprise supporting the other. The realities of basic survival in an unknown, sometimes hostile environment proved daunting to the settlers. Even the simple act of gathering ingredients to prepare a meal to feed a family was an enormous challenge. Without estab-lished farms and gardens, the staples of the home kitchen changed overnight, and foraging became the only option. The colonists were taught by the native people to hunt and fish, to

Natve Americans instructing settlers on planting techniques

Drawing by Palo Alto Pierce from Indian History and Genealogy *by Ebenezer W. Pierce, 1878*

fashion farm implements suited to the soils, and to plant, harvest and prepare these new fruits and vegetables.

In 1652, the settlers purchased a 104-square-mile area from the Wampanoag leader Massasoit. This original "Dartmouth Purchase" included what we now know as Acushnet, Fairhaven, New Bedford, Dartmouth, Westport, and parts of Tiverton and Little Compton. The land was divided into parcels, each 800 acres. These lands

Advertisement from the Bristol Gazette, *1812*

were further divided and sold to predominantly Quaker farmers. Quakers were persecuted in the Puritan Plymouth Colony, so many turned to the sparsely settled southern coast to make a life. Meanwhile, settlement continued east in townships through Wareham, and northwest from Fall River into central Massachusetts. These small townships were home to village mills, churches, slaughterhouses and liveries. General merchandise shops cropped up in central locations offering family farmers places to buy and sell.

These agrarian people grabbed hold of the Indian education they received in the planting of corn, squash and beans. They learned to identify wild herbs and various berries, and they sowed favorite plantings from the old country into this new earth. The solid agricultural foundation for this coastal region was built by courageous, hard-working settlers, together with Native Americans whose generosity and wisdom were crucial to the colonists' survival.

A new nation was born in this rich agricultural heritage, including the development of our regional cuisine. In the heavy black cauldrons of the settlers' kitchens, new recipes bubbled up. This blending of cultures became the pattern throughout American history. As new people and cultures arrived, their influence was reflected on the family dinner table and experienced with new ingredients and cooking techniques. New England's south coast melting pot eventually included French, Portuguese and Cape Verdean flavors, which we will visit in our third volume, *In the Neighborhood.*

The Heritage Farm Coast, like farmland everywhere, is threatened today by residential and commercial development due to population growth. However, this Great Farm is fighting back. Farmers, growers, entrepreneurs, and thoughtful citizens have joined together in farmers' co-ops, land trusts, land banks and regional resource groups. We as a community are looking ahead to revolutionize the farm, the marketplace, even the dinner table. This cookbook series is part of that venture.

In these pages, we begin with an overview from Bob Russell, who believes the region is poised for a sustainable future. Bob makes the indelible connection between our natural resources, our home lives, our bank accounts and our strength and stability as a region. Then we will explore some favorite spots on the Heritage Farm Coast circuit: Marie's herb gardens, David's hydroponic farm, Gray's Grist Mill and many others. I especially invite you to try (and experiment with) the recipes at the end of each section. Peter Bonome, farm planner, concludes with an account of his invaluable work. Peter is just one of many people working in dozens of groups to further the interest of the farmer and the region's quality of life. Enjoy the photographs, which offer glimpses of our beautiful area, then come, see and taste for yourself.

Moving Toward a Sustainable Future

By Robert James Russell II

As a youngster growing up in northern New Jersey, I witnessed the fantastically rapid loss of farmland to the pressing housing needs of post World War II families and their "boomers." The result was a megalopolis of one community blending into another. My heart was with the farmland and the loss of it bothered me.

In 1959, my wife Carol and I moved to Massachusetts to finish our schooling—she at Boston University and I at Harvard Business School. In 1963, we bought a home in Dighton and began raising our four children. In 1971, I was selected by area citizens to become president of the Environmental Protection Association of Southeastern New England, a group whose major effort questioned the need for the circumferential superhighway around Providence. These efforts and the people I came in touch with added greatly to my understanding of the region.

By profession I am a metallurgist and my career was in the field of clad metals, first with Texas Instruments in Attleboro, then with two partners in a small entrepreneurial high-technology clad metals business. In 1982, Carol and I made a momentous change in our lives, selling the clad metals business and buying the Smith Farm, where we established the Westport Rivers Vineyard and Winery. We chose the wine business because it was a career in which we could work together and also save and work a farm. Winemaking was my hobby. Family history helped out as well—Carol's father and grandfather had owned and operated the Germania Wine Cellars in Hammondsport, New York. Several years later, much to our joy, our two oldest sons joined the effort.

We chose Westport because the climate, the soils and the agricultural community suited our needs perfectly. We wanted to live and work in a close community where we could get help repairing tractors and purchasing plows. We did not want to embark on this endeavor in isolation.

In 1984, we witnessed the demise of several farms around us with concern, and considered selling the farm. Instead, we decided to stay, but with a renewed commitment, dedicating ourselves to the use and preservation of farmland. Carol became Open Space Committee chairperson of Westport and I initiated the start up of the Coastal Growers Association, today a cooperative of ninety farmers and twenty shellfishermen. By making this effort we believed we could help the region retain some of its farming ethos. We did not want to be the last historical farm.

Farmland preservation is the key to sustainability for ourselves and the region. Farmland provides a meaningful income to those who use it wisely as well as the beauty of open space, a dynamic financial engine, an improved tax base and a more sustainable environment. Unfortunately, contemporary planning and zoning methods and Chapter 61A tax relief will not preserve farmland. Only agricultural preservation restrictions (APR) or conservation easements will do the job.

What does "sustainable" mean? According to the World Commission on Environment and Development, presented by the Brundtland Commission, "Sustainable development is...to meet the needs of the present without compromising the ability of future generations to meet their own needs."

Our living environment is comprised of water, land and air. In comparison to the bulk of the earth and to outer space, our living environment is slight. This dimensional insignificance implies a certain susceptibility, a degree of fragility, conveyed in a simple and graphic way. Take an orange and let it represent the earth. Dip it into a bowl of water, remove it, and a thin residual film of water remains on the surface. This thin fragile film represents the living environment of the earth, where all of humankind resides.

Our region here in southeastern New England has an added environmental fragility because of the high ratio of water line length to land area. As an example, Westport has, at minimum, two miles of water line for every square mile of land, perhaps the highest in all of New England. The lands and waters in this region are intimately involved in a tug and pull as we use them for our benefit. We are communities on land connected by water and we live in symbiosis with the two. What we do to one environment affects the other.

Though we are surrounded by water, we cannot easily accumulate it for our use. Our topography is flat, and consequently there is little opportunity for the creation of reservoirs like Quabbin. It may come as a surprise to many that southeastern Massachusetts already has a shortfall of five million gallons per day. Economic development in Brockton has been inhibited for years by limited water resources.

We have water all around us and we can so easily pollute it. We see this in many ways: the oil drippings from our cars and trucks on driveways and roads find their way into our watersheds and aquifers; the draining of persistent toxins into the ocean spoils our harbors; septic systems leach a myriad of household chemicals and nitrogen into the groundwater supplies and nearby ponds and streams; the misuse of chemicals by farmers and others spoils the drinking water. Because of this intimate relationship between the lands and the waters, our region is more fragile than most. Imminent rapid development threatens both the land and the water. In *The Story of Civilization*, historian Will Durant observes that no society in the history of humankind has failed without having first spoiled its water supplies.

Land differs from water in the nature of its fragility. In most cases, when water is polluted, the pollution can be reversed or remedied. Water can be used and safely returned to the earth. Land is different. When land is polluted, leaving brownfields in its wake, it is extraordinarily difficult to reverse or remedy. And once farmland is used for development, it is impossible to reverse. Once land is gone, it is gone as a natural resource. In the last 30 years the region has lost one-third of its open space and farmland. The extent of further loss brings into question the issue of sustainability. What is the true loss to future generations?

A sustainable environment involves managing the land and water with practices that have long-term productive viability. The farmer who manages the soil for its total organic health needs fewer chemicals and gets greater productive output. This "healthy" farmland will provide sustainable production, thereby providing his generation and future generations with meaningful incomes. Sustainable production also applies to inshore and offshore waters that are managed wisely in terms of fishing methods and amount of catch. While management techniques are different from those for farmland, the outcomes are the same. The waters will continue to be productive for the long-term benefit of the fisherman. Our region is still enormously rich in land and water. Natural resources can provide the basis for powerful economic development. Their well managed use is sustainable development.

The President's Council on Sustainable Development issued a vision statement that stresses the importance of a growing economy that provides "equitable opportunities for satisfying livelihoods and a safe, healthy, high-quality life for current and future generations." A growing economy assumes a net financial capital gain within the region. Picture a small circle concentrically growing into a larger circle. The small circle represents the financial capital within the region today; the large circle, the future. Growth occurs if the dollar inflow is greater than the dollar outflow, a net gain of the financial capital of the region. An economy can grow in two major ways—from imported dollars and value-added dollars.

We import dollars when travelers and tourists from outside the region spend more money in the region than the region's own people spend outside. Or it occurs when the residents work outside their region, then spend and invest in their region. The major problem with the importation of dollars is the dependency upon the economies outside the region. The major strength is that things can happen quickly. A rail line can encourage people to live and spend here; an historic marine park, aquarium or national park can attract tourists.

Creating wealth from within the region is a second way to grow an economy. This can occur through the responsible use and harvest of natural resources, then adding value to these or other financial capital investments in the industrial, informational or virtual sectors of the economy. Think of an upside down triangle as a symbol of the economy. The apex represents the natural resources of the earth from which all wealth originates. Only four primary industries directly use these natural resources: farming, fishing, mining and forestry. Every dollar they generate multiplies itself five to seven times through the economy. No other industry does this. The wealth of all nations is based upon these four primary industries. The human brain applies knowledge and turns these natural resources into something of value. Inspired human ingenuity created the wheelbarrow, the automobile, the light bulb, the skyscraper, the computer, the laser, and the internet. The professional and supportive services—doctors, lawyers, bankers, entertainers, and service people—keep things going.

Idle equipment at Westport Vineyards

John K. Robson

Growing an economy from within is a powerful way for a region to become less dependent on the outside with more potential to achieve greater financial capital for the region. To sustain itself humankind needs these primary industries for food, clothing and shelter. Good stewardship and management practices must preside over these industries and their natural resources, with the goal of long-term and ongoing productive capacity. This region still has two active primary industries—farming and fishing. Combining these resources with the educational resources at UMass Dartmouth and other local educational institutions provides powerful economic opportunities.

Social capital is somewhat more qualitative and elusive than financial capital, but no less important. Good social capital exists when members of a community have a common set of goals and expectations, along with a shared set of values and a sense of trust that enables them to solve common problems. Poor social capital exists when people don't share similar values and don't trust each other. Two fishermen on the high seas will share weather information before an impending storm; two farmers will share a hay mower to avoid the double cost of each one owning a mower; doctors will share offices in a common building, and for security purposes neighbors will watch each other's homes.

The key words in social capital are common goals, shared values and trust. Social capital requires that leaders know the character and ethos of the people. They must listen, then turn their learning into some kind of action. For instance, the following may be said about this region:

We reside in the second and third most densely populated states in the country, yet residents have a sense of open space and quality of life because of the farms, the bodies of water and the forests—especially the Freetown State Forest and the Acushnet Cedar Swamp. The cities of Taunton, Fall River and New

Bedford have an enormously rich history which can be built upon for sustainability. The region has been chronically depressed for several generations and is desperate for a change. The area is culturally diverse.

The region has a mild climate—the sunniest and warmest in New England. While the Cape and the Islands can be called more temperate, they do not have as much sunlight because of the frequent fog conditions. We are one of the few regions in the United States that can lay claim to being a farm/fish, food/wine region. We have a plethora of farms and open spaces. Westport has the most dairy farms in the state. Bristol County is the number one county in vegetable production in Massachusetts.

Along Horseneck Road in Westport

John K. Robson

We have three important cities: New Bedford, the second most productive fishing port in poundage and the first in dollars in the United States in 1996; Fall River, still an active textile center and land-rich, with forests making up about fifty percent of its land area; Taunton, a diversified industrial center. The town of Westport boasts one of the most productive offshore lobster fleets in the United States, ranking about fifth.

The region has many fine restaurants attracting outstanding young chefs. The newly established International Culinary Institute in Fall River will graduate thousands of young people dedicated to the concept of wholesome, local cuisine.

We have six vineyards and three wineries, with one more winery on its way. If this region were in Europe, major portions of the farms and open spaces would be planted in vineyards. It is a premium chardonnay, riesling and sparkling wine (champagne) growing region, as Westport Rivers has demonstrated for the past five years.

Planners and leaders who know the region will be better able to understand the people. For their part, the people must help their leaders by offering their true and sincere thoughts. This valuable interplay will help maintain and enhance the social capital and improve the sustainability of the region.

Water harvesting on Decas Bros. cranberry bogs, South Carver

Tiverton homestead near Ferolbink Farm

Sustainability requires timely knowledge about subjects that are important to the people of a region. Using indicators (How are we doing today?) and benchmarks (What is the long-term projection?) we can measure our progress. Through evaluation, people will know if things are moving properly and whether their family's needs will be met in a responsible way. Citizens for a Sustainable Future will facilitate a process to bring a meaningful list of indicators and benchmarks to this region. This will be the first step on the road to having a sustainable region. We welcome you to join.

Robert James Russell II is president of Westport Rivers Vineyard and Winery. Citizens for a Sustainable Future met for the first time in New Bedford in the spring of 1998 to consider how the region might participate in a regional and global effort to work toward sustainability. Subsequent meetings have been facilitated by the Heritage Farm Coast Trust, a nonprofit organization, and held throughout the area. The group has broadly defined this region as the coastal watershed with the land mass from the Cape Cod Canal to the Sakonnet Passage in Rhode Island. Water is a common thread.

John K. Robson

Horseneck Road, Westport

Livestock at Westport Rivers Vineyard and Winery

John K. Robson

CHAPTER ONE

Herbs, Lettuces & Edible Flowers

*The ground is so fertile that questionless it is capable of any grain,
fruits, or seeds you will sow or plant…I made a garden on the top of
a rolling isle…in May that grew so well it served for sallets (salads)
in June and July.* —Captain John Smith, *New England's Trials*, 1614

Herbs, lettuces and edible flowers have been used for thousands of years to feed, to enhance and to heal. The explorers who perused this land before its colonization were obviously familiar with many culinary herbs and medicinal plants and found them in plenty here. Native Americans also identified and employed these natural resources for cooking and for use as medicines. For the most part, they were foraging, not farming them.

Rows of garlic chive flowers at Eva's Garden in Dartmouth

Joseph D. Thomas

Settlers raised, clipped and dried leaves and flowers to add a fresh flavor to winter meals. Beast and fowl were rubbed and stuffed with lavender, wild mint, sage and rosemary for savory fire-cooked meats. Salads of sorrel, purslane, chickweed and other leaves were dressed with a sprinkling of cider vinegar and salt. Squash blossoms were eaten raw and onion flowers were picked to season soups.

Edible nasturtium blossom

We sustained ourselves with alexander (horse parsley), and sorrel…and manie other herbs wherewith they make sallets. — M. John Brereton, 1602.

They also brought us some purslane, which grows abundantly among the Indian Corn and of which they take no more account than if it were a weed. — Samuel Champlain, 1605.

As the country grew, people abandoned the use of fresh herbs and flowers in cooking and medicines. Mass-produced dried herbs and spices took their place in grocery stores, providing easy year-round access, yet the flavor could not compare with fresh herbs and greens. Salads of fleshy purslane, bitter greens and sweet parsley were replaced by the hardhead iceberg lettuce and underripe tomato concoction duplicated in restaurants and home kitchens from coast to coast. After losing our connection to the subtle nuances of flavor offered by fresh herbs, lettuces and petals, we seem to be finding it again.

Culinary herbs, edible flowers and boutique and interesting lettuces are finally regaining their rightful place in the food world. Mixed baby greens salad or "mesclun mix" is available in grocery stores, and sprigs of fresh thyme and oregano are often found alongside them. Reports of the health value of common and unusual greens like the omega-3 packed

Greenhouses and rows of herbs at Eva's Garden

Joseph D. Thomas

purslane have sent gardeners and cooks to local nurseries and greenhouses to stock up. Use of flowers on restaurant plates to garnish and season is no longer unusual. Tender daylilies, perfumed rosa rugosa and pungent chive blossoms provide seasoning and decoration.

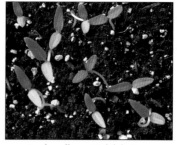

Basil seedlings, Oakdale Farm

Growers of fresh herbs and lettuces are finding a more secure and profitable market for their goods. Coastal Growers Association, the regional co-op, recognized the need for potted herbs, ornamental grasses, annuals, perennials and fall ornamentals, and formed a horticultural division that encourages members to expand and diversify their crops. In greenhouses, herb plantings are started early and some are ready for sale in late March. A single-crop farm has one harvest from which to profit, but the addition of herbs extends the season and cash flow improves. Fred Dabney, sales manager for the program, explains why it is so successful: "All the growers understand the need to maintain a similar level of quality and are committed to honoring their decided specs. Each one knows they are part of the whole. The member-growers of Coastal are producing some of the best herbs in New England."

Extending the season not only benefits the farmers, consumers reap the rewards of fresh, local goods during more of the year. Technology has provided the opportunity for some to grow fresh herbs and lettuces year-round through the farming technique known as hydroponics. A midwinter salad of three kinds of lettuce and tender herbs grown locally is now a reality. Marie Pray of Oakdale Farm and David Wilson of Salt Wind Farm, a hydroponic basil farm, will give an idea of the exciting present and future of specialty farming.

Cutting greens at Eva's Garden

The Oakdale Farm

As I crossed the Braga Bridge in Fall River to meet with Richard and Marie Pray in Rehoboth, I realized how unique our corner of New England really is. The invisible boundary between Massachusetts and Rhode Island does not interrupt the common feel of the coastal villages from Padanaram through Little Compton. The rural beauty of Dighton and Rehoboth blends easily into neighboring waterside Rhode Island towns. The two areas may be divided by water, but they share the common struggle to retain their identities in the face of rapid development. Oakdale Farm not only has managed to remain itself, but the Pray family has enjoyed some expansion over the years.

Richard and Marie Pray share an agricultural background that has helped them manage a bustling operation. Marie grew up in a farm family and worked in their farmstand. Richard led the farm life on the C.W. Pray Dairy Farm, the original family lands that Oakdale Farm now occupies. Richard manages the diverse crops that fill his 150 acres: sweet corn, collards, summer and winter squashes, lettuces, tomatoes, kale, cucumbers, hay and Indian corn. Why so many crops? His answer reflects the philosophy of many small farmers: "A (small) farmer can't concentrate on one crop. A bad year, you could get hurt. Variety makes the most of the seasons."

Marie Pray raises herbs, and her ten greenhouses overflow with culinary and medicinal herbs as well as perennial flowers. She pots the herbs in clay (for decoration or indoor growth) or in plastic for replants. Her growing venture keeps her running as she supplies local markets, farmstands and her own retail shop; she also participates in Coastal's horticulture programs. Twenty years' experience has served her well. "I learned from the old-timers and I love it. That's why I've done so well," she says.

Richard and Marie Pray outside their retail shop on the Oakdale Farm in Rehoboth

Joseph D. Thomas

Her customers are increasingly well-informed, she notes, about not only culinary herbs but medicinal and ornamental plantings too. She tends many varieties of rosemary, dill, oregano, basil and parsley year-round, but her buyers are also seeking the unusual. I was intrigued by the names and purported uses of some of the medicinal plants. Chamomile has long been used for its calming effects, and St. John's Wort is known for lifting the mood. Chewing on spilanthes might help numb a toothache and echinacea may be as broadly beneficial to general health as vitamin E. Betony, or "Lamb's Ear," is a beautiful plant with soft gray-green leaves. The leaves were commonly used in colonial times as an outer bandage. Lined with yarrow, a healing herb, Lamb's Ear was wrapped around a wound to protect and speed recovery.

Marie Pray

Marie is careful not to prescribe anything to customers. When someone asks about medicinal plants, she recommends they consult a good book and use such herbs responsibly.

Many of the plants are so attractive, they are commonly purchased as ornamentals. Valerian is a soft plant and it is lovely dried. Yarrow has been bred to grow in many colors, and creeping thymes make attractive borders.

Growing herbs has opened up opportunities for Marie Pray. She gives educational presentations at festivals, retail stores and conferences. Talking directly to her buyers gives her the chance to find out what they want and what new things she might try. This side of the family farm is growing and evolving, bringing with it the excitement of change.

The Prays have put much energy into reaching the public directly and their retail shop is in its tenth year. The barn is country comfortable with wood floors, dried wreaths and family treasures, including her grandfather's pumpkin scale. Shoppers can choose from gift items made by local artisans such as candles, wreaths and handcrafted furniture. Jars of homemade jellies, pickles and relishes made from traditional family recipes look glittering and delicious.

Basil plants at Oakdale, and (below) inside the Pray's retail shop

Joseph D. Thomas

Joseph D. Thomas

Visitors to Oakdale Farm can also connect with farm life through the Pray's unique brand of eco-tourism. Starting in mid September, hourly hay wagon tours led by "Farmer Brown" travel on a path through the woods to the pumpkin patch, then head on to greet the animals. Chico the rooster, Babe the pig, Winnie the goat and the cows Nellie, Ben and Jerry greet their guests and accept an occasional apple for a snack. The trip ends at a maze constructed of 200 bales of hay. Weekday tours are filled with local school children; the weekends are booked for birthday parties. Evening hay rides geared toward families take place during the Christmas season. Richard and Marie Pray are always there and involved. They want to be the faces people see when they come to the farm.

The Prays have seen many of their neighbors lose or let go of their farms. In some cases, their children did not want to carry on the farming tradition and their land was sold to developers. The profit was used for their retirement. Marie and Richard believe the "new farmer," a recent arrival on the scene, is in it for the long term. "There are two types of farmers," said Marie, "those who work hard and those who work smart." Richard and Marie hope they are doing it right, working hard and smart.

Chico (top), the family pet, and painted pumpkins decorate the landscape at Oakdale Farm.

Inside an Oakdale greenhouse

Salt Wind Farm

Hydroponics is "the growing of plants in nutrient solutions," according to Webster. This wonderfully simple definition is only a "how-do-you-do" introduction to the realities of this unique type of farming. When I first visited Salt Wind Farm in Dartmouth, it was a chilly, damp November day. The physical makeup of this large hydroponic farm struck me as rather uncomplicated, basically contained acreage. I stepped inside the great rectangular greenhouse out of the raw wind into early summer. The air was warm and moist, filled with the heady aroma of fresh basil and organic matter. The low hum of fans seemed to circulate the peaceful quiet of growing plants. I scanned the tidy rows of pvc-pipe, admiring the order of it all: bright green basil plants growing in "peer groups," at different stages of development. I knew about hydroponics, but had never actually experienced or understood it. Standing in the center of that place filled with growth, warmth and life, while outside a cold wind blew through leafless trees under a gray sky, I began to understand.

Meeting owner David Wilson completed the picture for me. This indoor farm is an extension of the person himself, reflecting his master's degree in chemical engineering from MIT; his work as an engineer for an international oil and gas company; his experience as director of research and development for New England's largest grower of alfalfa and bean sprouts. Salt Wind Farm is a unique creation, growing out of David's love of the scientific method (controlled experimentation), combined with his desire to make things grow, topped by his fierce determination to support regional agriculture from vegetable and dairy farms to herbs to wineries to hydroponics.

The process of hydroponic farming seeks to eliminate certain unpredictables usually associated with farming. Basil seeds are sown into a small cube of synthetic foam and set in a germination area. The plant will now grow in an open-irrigation system of split pvc-pipe and recycled water. When the sprout appears, the rotation cycle begins; the plants are moved further apart as the size increases. Water and temperature are controlled by a complex computer system.

Large fans keep the air circulating so the temperature remains around 80° during the day and no lower than 60° at night. The roof is covered with a double layer of heavy plastic that is filled with outside air.

What are the results of such technical precision? Pesticides are almost never used as the life of the succulent basil plant is

Hydroponic basil seedlings at Salt Wind Farm

John K. Robson

so short and a pest's only access to them is through the roof. Waste is minimal. All the unusable organic material is composted. Quality and consistency are more easily controlled in this environment, and the shelf life is a bit longer than the traditionally grown, a big help when it comes to shipping and storage. David Wilson is at home with the science of "controlled environment agriculture." His biggest challenge is in the "arts and crafts" of it.

"Nature works on an undetermined number of variables," he says. David can manipulate the weather conditions, but color, flavor and texture are up to the plant. When we last spoke, he was researching Mediterranean soils and climate. A basil plant is what it eats. The right diet will encourage full flavor, rich color and tender yet sturdy leaves. How can each trait be developed without losing the others? Finding answers to these questions by experimenting presents an exciting challenge to his engineering mind. David Wilson is also confronted with occasional setbacks. A diseased batch of seeds may appear normal upon arrival and through early growth, then reveal itself well into the plant's maturity. All that can be retrieved is experience and learning. His pursuit to satisfy an ever-rising set of standards keeps pushing and testing.

The growth of this business has been an exciting ride for Mr. Wilson. He began by trying several different vegetables and herbs, lettuces, cucumbers and tomatoes. The decision to focus on basil was a recent one. David felt that the Northeast market holds enough demand for this "finesse" herb. Mediterranean cooking has grown in popularity and more people who cook at home have discovered the difference fresh basil makes in their favorite pasta dish.

What will determine the success of indoor, computerized farming? Consumer education. Getting the word out and letting shoppers and cooks discover for themselves what this product has to offer. To that end, David Wilson will continue to board his agricultural spaceship, watch over his plants and seek to uncover the mysteries in the world of nature.

Young basil plants at Salt Wind Farm

John K. Robson

Handling Tips

George Farm iceberg lettuce

All fresh lettuces and herbs, whether organic or not, should be washed and spun dry thoroughly before using them. If you do not own a salad spinner, I encourage you to purchase one as they are inexpensive and do the job well. Though I have heard of people filling clean socks with washed greens and spinning them overhead, or tying up a towel of wet lettuce and running it through the spin cycle of the washing machine, I recommend a simple salad spinner. When purchasing fresh lettuces and herbs, check the leaves and stems for signs of slime or browning.

Edible flowers should be purchased from a reputable grower or picked from your own yard. Do not eat anything sprayed with chemicals or picked by a busy roadside. Some tasty, easy-to-find-or-grow flowers are daylilies, beach roses, tulips, johnny jump-ups and nasturtiums. Flowering herbs are also easy to cut and usually quite tasty. Keep all lettuces and herbs cool and dry in the refrigerator. Local lettuces and herbs grown outdoors are available May through October; hydroponic greens and herbs are available all year.

For everyone who has to trim back a rambunctious herb garden, but can't always find a use for their cuttings, I give you…

Cuttings Broth

Organic herb gardener Eva Sommaripa of Dartmouth encouraged me to experiment with stocks using this very simple procedure.

Fill a stock pot with clean herb garden trimmings such as sweet cicely, fennel, basil, parsley, serpent garlic, thyme, mint, rosemary and chives.

Fill the pot with water to the level of the herbs, set it over a high flame and bring it to a boil. Simmer for several minutes. Shut it off and let it steep for about 10 minutes. Strain the herbs out and drop into your compost. Chill the stock down and use it to make hot or cold soups, sauces, or to steam vegetables, poached meat or fish.

YIELD BASED ON POT SIZE.

Eva cutting herbs

Tossed Salad

I find lettuces grown indoors to be tender and milder in flavor than their outdoor counterparts. The leaves need a light rinse and spin, but there is no need to soak them. It is best to wash them just prior to use and store the head whole in its package in the refrigerator.

Our fridge is rarely home to bottled dressings, with the exception of a few good specialty brands. I toss our salads by drizzling oil around the edge of the salad bowl, followed by the verjus or vinegar, a sprinkling of salt, then folding it all together by hand, tasting and adjusting. Our homemade dressings resemble the verjus Vinaigrette and Marinade *(page 115) with a tablespoon of mustard or sour cream whisked in to the verjus, followed by the oil. Verjus is the freshly pressed juice from underripe grapes that have been pruned from vines to encourage better quality grapes for wine. French in origin and pronounced* vayr-shzoo, *it is nonalcoholic and unfermented.*

Spring, summer and fall, combine indoor and outdoor lettuces with a mixture of herbs and other greens like cilantro, parsley, basil, purslane, young mustard greens, mizuna, sorrel, sweet cicely and spinach. In winter, I use local hydroponic basil and lettuce together and cut some potted herbs to spruce up my vinaigrette.

George's red lettuce

Purslane Salad

A wonderfully simple recipe that uses some delicate and flavorful herbs.

Combine the purslane, jicama and peppers, then toss in enough vinaigrette to coat the leaves. Refrigerate remaining vinaigrette to use as a marinade for meats or fish, or for the next salad.

MAKES 4 TO 6 SIDE PORTIONS.

Tim Partridge, Chef, East Coast Grill, Cambridge, MA

Rows of lettuces, including red russian kale, at John George Farm

John K. Robson

1 cup purslane sprigs and
   chopped stems
1 cup julienned (very thin strips)
   jicama (you can substitute
   fennel, cucumber or celery)
½ cup julienned red or green
   pepper
Combine and serve with:

LIME VINAIGRETTE
Combine:
¼ cup fresh lime juice (lemon
   juice may be substituted)
1 cup very good olive oil
1 tbsp. chopped fresh garlic
1 tbsp. chopped fresh cilantro
   (or substitute Italian parsley,
   orange mint or lemon balm)

Pesto

½ cup canola oil
6–8 cloves garlic, peeled
⅓ cup nuts (I use what I have—
    pecans, walnuts and pine
    nuts work the best.)
3 oz. good parmesan cheese,
    cut into ¼" chunks
2 cups basil leaves, picked and
    washed
1 cup flat parsley leaves, picked
    and washed
Extra virgin olive oil

Basil

My husband Paul, a former apprentice of Guiliano Bugiali in Florence, Italy, learned to make pesto (paste) in its homeland. This version uses the most common ingredients: basil, olive oil, and garlic. I use this pesto directly over cooked pasta, stirred into mayonnaise spread on a deli or chicken sandwich, shaken into a simple vinaigrette, or spooned onto slices of fresh tomato in a BLT.

In a blender or food processor, pulse the canola oil, garlic, nuts and cheese to make a paste. Drop in the basil and parsley and pulse them in, adding the olive oil in small amounts until the mixture becomes a smooth paste, the consistency of thick paste. Be careful not to overblend or the color will change quickly from brilliant to army green.

The pesto should be stored tightly covered in the refrigerator for up to one week. Freeze in ice cube trays, then tightly bag and store frozen to add a bit of summer to a winter soup or sauce.

MAKES ABOUT 1½ CUPS.

Brunch Eggs

¼ cup olive oil
½ lb. linguica, chourico, or any
    robust sausage, cooked and
    crumbled
4 scallions, thinly sliced
1 tbsp. chopped parsley
6 eggs
¼ cup milk or cream
1 tbsp. sweet cicely, chopped
Salt and pepper
Hot sauce, optional

Chopped olives, sautéed garlic and mushrooms, or any fresh herbs would be delicious additions to this dish. Sweet cicely is a feathery herb with a delicate anise taste. The flowers and seed pods are also edible and are stronger and sweeter than the leaves.

Preheat oven to 425°. Pour the oil in a 9" casserole or glass pie dish and set in the oven. Beat the eggs with the milk, salt, pepper and a few shakes of hot sauce, if you like food with a kick. Remove the warmed dish from the oven, cover the bottom with the sausage, scallions, cicely and parsley, then pour the eggs over the top. Bake until puffed and golden around the edges, about 15–20 minutes, and allow to sit for several minutes. Slice in wedges and serve with sour cream, salsa or warm tomato sauce.

MAKES 4 SERVINGS.

Purslane and Tarragon with Thick Garlicky Yogurt

Let yogurt sit in a coffee filter fit into a strainer over a bowl for 1 hour. All the water should run out and the yogurt should be thick like sour cream. Place chopped garlic in a mixing bowl with the lemon juice and salt. Let stand for about 10 minutes. Stir in yogurt, olive oil and pepper. Wash and dry purslane and tarragon using a salad spinner. Roughly chop and add to yogurt. Fold in carrot and cucumber and reseason. Serve right away.

MAKES 6 SERVINGS.

Ana Sortun, Executive Chef, Casablanca, Cambridge, MA

2 cups yogurt
4 small cloves garlic, chopped
   fine or through a garlic press
2 tbsp. very good olive oil
2 tbsp. fresh squeezed lemon
   juice
¼ tsp. fresh ground black pepper
4 cups packed purslane sprigs
¼ cup packed tarragon leaves
1 carrot, grated
1 English cucumber, peeled and
   seeded, then grated
Kosher or sea salt to taste

Rows of violas at Eva's Garden in Dartmouth

Joseph D. Thomas

Grilled Leg of Lamb
with Honey-Lavender Marinade and
Grilled Ratatouille with Oregano Oil

Leg of lamb, boned and
    butterflied

MARINADE:
⅓ cup olive oil
6 shallots, chopped
4 cloves garlic, chopped
1 sprig thyme
2 sprigs lavender
2 tbsp. black pepper, coarse
    ground
¼ cup honey
¼ cup fresh lemon juice
1 tsp. salt

RATATOUILLE:
1 eggplant
2 small zucchini
2 tomatoes
2 red onions
2 tbsp. garlic, roasted
Olive oil as needed
Salt and pepper to taste

OREGANO OIL:
½ cup washed oregano leaves
1 cup olive oil, pomace or extra
    virgin

FOR THE MARINADE:
Sauté the shallots and garlic in olive oil over medium-high heat until soft. Add remaining ingredients off the heat and blend well. Rub into lamb. Keep covered in refrigerator overnight. Heat grill to medium. Place lamb on grill, cook for 10 minutes on each side or until internal temperature is 140°. Remove to platter, let rest at least 10 minutes before slicing.

FOR THE RATATOUILLE:
Slice all vegetables ¾" thick. Drizzle with olive oil, salt and pepper. Place on hot grill and cook on both sides until vegetables are softened slightly. Remove from grill and chop coarsely. Toss in a bowl with the garlic and season with salt and pepper to taste.

FOR THE OREGANO OIL:
Pulse oregano and olive oil in food processor. Remove to a nonreactive bowl and cover. Let sit at room temperature for several hours. Strain through cheesecloth. Store refrigerated.

To serve, slice lamb and set on a bed of ratatouille. Drizzle with oregano oil. (The oil can be made a day ahead while the lamb is marinating).

MAKES 10–12 SERVINGS.

Mike Melo, M & C Restaurant, New Bedford, MA

Garlic Chive Blossoms

John K. Robson

Great Hill Blue Cheese on
Eva's Wild Greens with Peppered Pears

This salad utilizes a few of the many wonderful local products that are found in southeastern Massachusetts: Great Hill Farms Blue Cheese in Marion, Dartmouth organic grower Eva Sommaripa's wild greens, and a sweet white dessert wine. Tim would suggest assembling both the peppered pears and the vinaigrette ahead of time, preferably the morning before your dinner.

FOR THE PEARS:

In a saucepan, combine vanilla, wine and water. Start with the liquid as cold as possible. Bring to a simmer and cook the pears for 10 minutes. Remove the pears from the liquid and let them cool. Bring the liquid to a boil and reduce it until you have about one cup of liquid left or until it has a syrup consistency. Reserve this—you'll need to add it to the vinaigrette.

Coat the flesh side of the cooled pears with the sugar and cracked black pepper. Preheat a sauté pan, add the butter and the pears, flesh side down. Cook for about 5 minutes or until the sugar caramelizes. Remove from the pan and place on a plate, flesh side up. Hold in the refrigerator until ready to serve.

FOR THE VINAIGRETTE:

Place the vinegar, cider, mustard, shallots and honey in a mixing bowl. Whisk in the cooled poaching liquid, then slowly add the olive oil until the mixture is emulsified. Adjust the seasonings with salt and pepper to your own taste. Refrigerate until ready to serve.

TO ASSEMBLE:

Portion the greens equally onto 6 chilled plates. You can either grill the pears or place them in a preheated 400° oven until heated through. Once they're hot, cut them into fans and place on top of the salad. Place the cheese on the salad. Drizzle about ¼ cup of vinaigrette over each salad and serve immediately. In warmer months you can serve the pears cold. Just make sure to caramelize the sugar well when you sauté them.

MAKES 6 GENEROUS SALADS.

Timothy Quinn, Executive Chef, Not Your Average Joe's, Dartmouth, MA

FOR THE PEARS:
6 fresh pears, cut in half and cored
3 oz. pure vanilla extract
1 cup sweet, white dessert wine
1½ cups water
2 tbsp. black peppercorns, cracked by hand, or coarse cracked pepper
Granulated sugar
6 oz. unsalted butter

FOR THE VINAIGRETTE:
1 cup apple cider vinegar
½ cup fresh apple cider
2 oz. Dijon mustard
1 oz. chopped shallots
2 oz. honey
1 cup reserved liquid from the poached pears
2 cups olive oil
Salt and pepper to taste

TO ASSEMBLE:
6 generous handfuls fresh, local greens
Caramelized pears
Vinaigrette
6 oz. blue cheese cut into 6 slices

Mizuna and radicchio

John K. Robson

Spicy Codfish Cakes with Cilantro Aioli

For the Cilantro Aioli:
1 bunch cilantro, washed, stems removed
Grated zest and juice from 1 large lemon
4 cloves garlic, coarsely chopped
½ cup mayonnaise, preferably reduced fat
1 head green leaf lettuce, washed and dried, tough stems removed
1 large ripe mango or papaya, peeled, pitted/seeded and cut into thin strips
⅓ cup mint leaves
1 lime, cut into wedges

For the Fish Cakes:
1 lb. boneless/skinless cod fillet
2 green onions, minced
1 jalapeño pepper, cored, seeded and minced
1 tbsp. minced garlic
1 tbsp. minced ginger
1 tbsp. Thai fish sauce or soy sauce
Grated zest of one lemon
Peanut oil, for cooking

For the Cilantro Aioli:

Coarsely chop the cilantro leaves and put in a food processor. Add the lemon zest and garlic, process until finely chopped. Add the mayonnaise and process until the cilantro is flecked in the mayonnaise. Add the lemon juice and pulse to mix. Transfer the cilantro aioli to a serving bowl and set it on a platter with the lettuce leaves, mango, mint leaves and lime wedges. Cover with plastic wrap and refrigerate.

For the Fish Cakes:

Cut the fish into 1" pieces and finely chop it in food processor 10–20 seconds. In a bowl, combine the fish, green onions, jalapeño, garlic, ginger, fish sauce and lemon zest and stir until blended. Form the fish mixture into patties of about 2 tablespoons each; you should have 16 patties.

Pour about ⅛" oil into a large frying pan. Heat over medium-high heat until ripples develop in the oil. Carefully slide patties into pan using a spatula. Cook until golden on the bottom, 2–4 minutes. Turn and cook until golden on the bottom and opaque in the center. Repeat to cook the remaining patties, adding more oil to pan as needed.

Pile the fish cakes onto the serving platter alongside the other ingredients. To eat, put a fish cake, some mango and mint in the center of a lettuce leaf. Sprinkle with a squeeze of lime, then spoon on some of the cilantro aioli. Fold up and eat out of hand.

Serves 4 (or 8 first-course portions).

Michael Frady, Chef, The Barn, Adamsville, RI

Workers at Ward's Berry Farm

Joseph D. Thomas

Grilled Honey and Lavender
Dartmouth Scallops on Eva's Pea Greens

Up to two days ahead of time, chop the lavender and add to the olive oil. Cover and let stand at room temperature.

Mix the infused oil with the honey, wine, and black pepper. Place the scallops in a glass dish. Pour the liquid over the scallops. Cover and refrigerate the scallops for at least 8 hours.

Remove the scallops from the marinade. Reserve marinade. Prepare a charcoal grill. When the coals are ready, place a metal screen on top of your grate and grill the scallops until they are cooked through. You could also skewer the scallops and place them on your regular grate.

Place the leftover marinade in a small skillet. Over low heat bring to a simmer. Whisk in the rice wine vinegar and adjust the seasonings with salt and pepper to taste.

Place the washed pea tendrils on 6 plates. Place equal amounts of scallops on each plate and drizzle the vinaigrette over the top. Serve immediately.

MAKES 6 SERVINGS.

Timothy Quinn, Executive Chef, Not Your Average Joe's, Dartmouth, MA

3 tbsp. fresh lavender, flowers and leaves
¼ cup olive oil
½ cup wildflower honey
½ cup sweet, white dessert wine
1 tbsp. cracked black peppercorns
3 lbs. Dartmouth scallops (six 8-oz. portions)
1½ lbs. fresh pea tendrils or substitute fresh arugala
¼ cup rice wine vinegar
Remaining marinade from the scallops

John K. Robson

Scarlet runner beans

Hopi red dye amaranth with other herbs and flowers at Eva's Garden

Joseph D. Thomas

Basic Pizza Dough

1½ tsp. active dry yeast
1½ tsp. honey or molasses
1 tbsp. olive or canola oil
1 cup water, body temperature
3½ cups all-purpose flour
1½ tsp. salt

Combine the yeast, honey, oil and water and let stand 10 minutes. In a mixer with dough hook, or large-capacity food processor, pour the liquid, flour and salt together and combine to form a ball, smooth to touch, not tacky. Set in an oiled bowl and cover. Allow to rise to double its size in a warm place.

Note: See note on page 119 for making dough.

Lovage Breads

1 batch pizza dough (see recipe for "Basic Pizza Dough"), cut into 6 equal-size pieces
1 qt. heavy cream
8 sprigs lovage with hefty stems
White wine
1 16-oz. can strained plum tomatoes roughly chopped or small box of Pomi tomatoes
1 cup grated parmesan cheese
Salt and freshly ground pepper to taste

This is a signature dish at Casablanca. It is served with grilled lamb, artichoke caponata, and minted couscous.

Boil cream and lovage with a splash of white wine until cream is reduced more than half and is thick. Use a very heavy pan with a capacity of at least 3 quarts. It will boil over easily while reducing, so watch it. Strain through a sieve and whisk in the tomatoes. Stir in the parmesan cheese and season with salt and pepper. Preheat oven to 350°. Sprinkle cookie sheet with cornmeal. Roll out one of the 6 balls of dough to ½" thick in a free-form shape. Spread some of the lovage mixture evenly on the dough. Bake until bubbly and crisp. Cool for several minutes before slicing and serving.

MAKES 6 LARGE BREADS.

Ana Sortun, Executive Chef, Casablanca, Cambridge, MA

Stone wall along Route 77 in Tiverton

John K. Robson

Lemon Rosemary Cookies

Preheat oven to 325°. With an electric mixer, cream butter and sugar until fluffy. Add eggs and beat in thoroughly. Fold in lemon rind and rosemary. Sift together flour, salt and baking powder. Fold into the egg/batter mixture. Drop by small spoonfuls onto parchment-lined cookie sheet. Flatten with cup dipped in sugar. Bake for 7 minutes.

MAKES ABOUT 2 DOZEN.

Donna Macomber, The Provender, Tiverton Four Corners, RI

1 cup sugar
3 tbsp. butter, softened
2 eggs, well beaten
3 tsp. lemon rind
1 tbsp. rosemary, chopped fine
1½ cups flour
¼ tsp. salt
2 tsp. baking powder

Daylily Cheesecake

The good people of Tranquil Lake Nursery in Rehoboth introduced me to the delicacy of daylily petals. They encouraged me to stroll through their field of lilies, an ocean of color, filled with hundreds of varieties. Each lily had its own texture and sweetness. I enjoy experimenting with them in the kitchen. This creamy, not-too-sweet cheesecake glides easily over the palate. The petals in the cake give a confetti-like appearance.

Daylilies can also be filled with an herbed cream cheese mixture and served whole, as an appetizer. The petals are also easily tossed in a dinner salad.

Preheat oven to 325°. Coat a 9" cake pan with nonstick spray. Beat the cream cheese with an electric mixer on high speed until fluffy. Stream in the sugar and beat until dissolved. Beat the eggs in one at a time on medium speed. Reduce the speed to low and stream in the extract, then the half-and-half until completely incorporated. Fold the daylily petals in with a wooden spoon. Pour the batter into the prepared pan. Set into a shallow roasting pan and fill with warm water at least halfway up the outside of the cake pan. Bake for 1 hour or until the center is just set. Chill until completely cooled. Remove by setting the pan in a shallow bowl of warm water for about 10 seconds and turning out onto a plate. Instead of slicing the cheesecake, spoon it right out of the pan into a daylily or serve in a dessert dish with fresh berries and crispy cookies.

MAKES ONE 9" CHEESECAKE.

1 lb. cream cheese, softened
¾ cup granulated sugar
4 eggs, room temperature
2 tsp. pure vanilla or almond extract
1 cup half-and-half
2 cups daylily petals, thinly sliced

Betse Downey

Daylillies at Tranquil Lake Nursery

CHAPTER TWO

Pumpkins, Squash & Potatoes

The men…brought us little squashes as big as a fist, which we ate as a
salad like cucumbers and they were very good. —Samuel Champlain, 1605

Askutasquash, the Narragansett Indian word for squash of any variety literally means "something that is eaten raw." Native people thrived on squash, corn and beans and taught the settlers how to plant, harvest and handle them. These "three sisters" became a staple of the settlers. (See Chapter Three.) Squash, including the pumpkin, is a New World food and actually a fruit. Native Americans sowed squash seeds at the base of a corn planting and the vines spread out over the ground to ripen. The harvest of the squash was later than corn, so valuable land space was not wasted.

Autumn harvest display at Westport Fair

John K. Robson

Yellow crooknecks, pumpkins and many other varieties of summer squash were common to the Native American farmer, as were butternut and acorn in the winter variety. Summer varieties were generally eaten raw, while the winter squash were buried in hot ash to roast or boiled in a pot of game stew.

Europe had some squash-like vegetables but none quite like what the settlers found around Plymouth Colony. The winter squash possessed long-term storage qualities, another gift of survival to the settlers. The Native Americans bred several varieties to serve certain purposes; some stored better than others or could thicken a soup more quickly. Colonists adopted their thrifty farming techniques, planting squash and corn together, as well as cooking these new vegetables. They were undaunted by the seemingly impenetrable skins of the pumpkins and butternuts.

The thick, sweet flesh of a roasted butternut could be eaten plain or scooped into a batter of cornmeal and eggs for a tasty pudding or cake. Summer squash were eaten un-cooked and enjoyed during their growing season.

Again, the health benefits of native produce saved the colonists; winter squash are full of vitamin A and fiber. At a time of year when nothing was fresh, the hearty vegetable was still as good as the day it was harvested.

New Englanders love their traditional buttered mash, creamy pumpkin pie and smooth squash soups. New varieties have emerged and the selections available to growers are in the hundreds. Westport farmer Paul Costa is a serious squash grower, a solid resource for the traditional and an experimenter of the unusual. A look at his family farm gives us a glimpse of the past and hope for the future.

Also in every island …are a great store of groundnuts…These nuts we found to be as good as potatoes. —Notes on Gosnold's Expedition, 1605

Baby pumpkins, Westport Fair

John K. Robson

White-fleshed potatoes had an interesting bounce about the oceans before becoming part of American farming and culinary cultures. Sweet potatoes were native to the New World, but South America was the point of origin for the white potato.

Sir Francis Drake carried the tuber from Cartagena, Colombia back to England to be presented to Queen Elizabeth. The potato never actually hit her plate, as the vegetable was discarded and the greens were cooked and served instead. This might explain why it is a little-mentioned crop in our early history. Obviously, Bartholomew Gosnold's men were well-enough acquainted with the vegetable to compare the flavor to that of roasted ground-nuts (a member of the pea family).

The potato was grown in Europe toward the end of the 16th century, but mostly for its appearance, not as a crop. The tubers' deepest root was in Ireland and they were grown in quantity by the late 16th and early 17th centuries, thus giving the vegetable its Irish identity. By the mid 1700s, they were being planted in the Connecticut Valley as a staple crop.

When cooked, the white potato was generally boiled (at one time they were thought to be poisonous until toxins were removed by boiling) or baked in the ashes of a cooling oven. Their contribution to early regional cookery was minimal, but the potato was another crop that became acclimated to our climate and soil. Although less rocky soil is ideal, waterside farmland has the benefit of moderate temperatures so frost damage to the plants is minimized. Dampness can present a fungus problem and too much rain can expose the tubers to sunlight, causing a greenish cast to the vegetable. Much of New England's relationship to the baking potato was developed in the state of Maine.

The traditional baking potato, although delicious, has had to share market space with some rejuvenated heirloom and new varieties. With exciting names like Yukon Gold, Rose Blush, Fingerling and Green Mountain, specialty and Old World potatoes are a hot item on contemporary restaurant menus. This emerging interest in variety means boutique vegetable growers can expand their repertoire and large growers have a market for "just for fun" crops.

Potato rows at Ward's Berry Farm

Joseph D. Thomas

Costa Farm

The farming life does something to a person, inside and out. It colors the blood, weathers the face, is worn like gloves on the hands. When one responds to the call of farming and uses his gifts and talents to the fullest, it shapes his character, giving him a strength and assurance that seems always in forward motion. Such is the description of Paul Costa, whose life energy flows into his rambling farm, located on Main Road in Westport. The personification of kinetic energy, Paul is driven to fulfill his destiny—to plant seeds, watch them grow, brood over their fruit and deliver them into the hands and homes of his community. Contrary to much of society today, Paul does not equate success with the ability to buy things. Rather, he measures success by reaching personal bests.

This code of life determines the "hows" and "whats" regarding his 75-acre family farm. Costa's crops are as varied as most farmers who sell from their own stand. His emphasis is on squash and pumpkins. Lush patches of leafy jack be little and sugar pie pumpkins, spaghetti, delicata and blue hubbard squash border rows of butternut and sweet dumplings. The nine varieties of corn reflect Paul's desire to keep experimenting with big crops. Peas, beans, lettuces, onions, carrots, potatoes and tomatoes (including several unique heirloom varieties) are grown to sell to his neighbors at his stand, to Coastal Growers or directly to local businesses.

Expansion and experimentation keep things interesting for Paul Costa. He set up a greenhouse to start his own plants and will use it to raise flowers and herbs as well. His love for robust foods and flavors brought him into the world of boutique peppers. Some of the most beautiful and most biting varieties are his favorites. He can grow almost anything, he says, but the question, "Who will buy it?" comes first.

Paul Costa harvesting peppers

John K. Robson

Reaching the public palate is a priority for this farmer. In his opinion, mass-production farming and the move toward year-round availability of just about everything has dulled the country's collective taste buds. His direct, hands-on approach to life also extends to marketing. If a shopper pulls into his lot and does not find the super-sweet variety of corn she wants, this farmer offers an ear or two of something different to try at home. He sends people on their way with an "I'll see you tomorrow for more!" The Costa confidence is most often affirmed.

"A farmer has to be an educator," he says. The statement is direct and his tone defies argument. Every year Mr. Costa leads a seed-to-produce workshop for Westport kindergarten classes, teaching the children about planting, waiting and watching. Three to four weeks later, the eager students descend on the Costa farm, bringing along the plants they have been caring for, so they can dig in the dirt to give their precious cargo a more permanent home. The reality of where their favorite fruits and vegetables come from is placed literally in their little hands. Paul says the results of this are immediate and, he hopes, long-term.

Paul shares with others the delight he receives in picking what he grows. Children with learning disabilities are part of his yearly harvesting team. The work is physically demanding and requires patience, and these young people put forth a consistent effort in every task, including the most tedious. Their energy is an inspiration to him as they come and go each day with the same enthusiasm.

The pressures of economics and government regulation are as intense on the Costa farm as on all of his neighbors. The reality a small farmer faces, competing for market space with corporate giants on cheaper land, with overseas crops and abundant labor, is only one concern. Pest and disease control becomes more problematic as restrictions become more stringent. Are there any answers to these very big problems?

"The only salvation I see is cooperative strength," says Paul Costa. The old-fashioned sense of community that supports itself and creates a sound base for growth must reinvent itself, and today's market must be redefined. Old ways and values are part of this, but only part. Advances in integrated pest management (IPM) are providing some immediate help to crops at risk of poor nutrition and infestation. A harmless soap-like soil enhancer worked into a pumpkin patch yields a stronger crop; refined soil testing procedures tell Paul if his plants are receiving the valuable nitrogen they need at crucial points during growth and ripening.

I asked Paul's opinion of the current push toward reclaiming open space through land banking, preservation efforts and trusts. Paul Costa acknowledges the value in these strategies but he would include an educational aspect too. "If we save farmland, who will farm it? Funding agricultural programs in schools (at all levels) would promote farming as an occupation." However, Paul says he meets young people who are inclined to farming but not so sure about the financial picture and the "hard life" of personal sacrifice. His research into ancient cultures reveals a striking similarity to our economic climate now. A powerful empire is built on the farming of land, animals and the sea. The pursuit of affluence and the ethereal take the place of tilling the soil, and farming is abandoned. The empire becomes food-dependent and therefore vulnerable. It eventually falls.

Despite this bleak observation, Paul Costa will not give up. He will stay involved and push forward because this is who he is. "Do you love it?" I asked, as I got ready to go. He replied soberly, "My answer varies moment to moment, depending on the circumstances." Then he smiled, "I will do this until I die."

Ferolbink Farm

The stretch of countryside that connects Four Corners in Tiverton to Little Compton, Rhode Island, is a lovely mosaic of charming storefronts, classic New England homes and open fields. Near the point where the two towns merge is the home of Ferolbink Farms. Just follow the "pick-your-own blueberries" sign on the right. The property is a study in early and contemporary American farming. A beautiful old house sits up near the road and a brand-spanking new one rests comfortably in the fields, surrounded by spectacular views. Road-weary pickup trucks parked along the wall of an enormous storage barn contrast dramatically to the trailer trucks ready for loading nearby. A walk up the drive, past the equipment sheds, past a graveyard for tractor parts that have given well over the years, leads to the crest of a hill that faces southeast. A meticulous quilt of fields rolls downward, its hem dipping into the waters of the Sakonnet River and Narragansett Bay. It is breathtaking.

Owner Pete Peckham runs the 500 plus-acre-farm, founded in 1944 by his parents, Ferol and Bernard "Bink" Peckham. To say that farming was a career choice for Pete would probably bring a smile to his lips. "I was born into it," he told me. "I could not imagine my life any other way." If I had met Pete when he was a young boy, I believe that statement would be the same. When the time came for college, his choice was to go to the University of Maryland and earn his degree in agronomy. Today his farm and family are his delight. He and his wife have four children. Kari, the youngest, in her late teens, loves to help and get her hands dirty.

Most of the crops raised on Ferolbink Farm with its 325 acres (plus 200 leased) are fairly traditional: pumpkins, butternut and acorn squash, 300 blueberry bushes, tomatoes, onions, 15 acres of sweet corn and six to seven acres of Christmas trees. All of this repre-

Pete Peckham plowing at Ferolbink

Joseph D. Thomas

sents only 10 percent of the overall production. Their largest crop is potatoes. A few of the varieties they grow are reds, russets, Yukon gold and Green Mountain, but eight out of every 10 potatoes they raise are for potato chips! The difference between chip potatoes and those we simmer in soup, bake twice, and roast is like night and day. Frying potatoes are bred specifically to have high "solids," less moisture, less shrinkage and a consistent size.

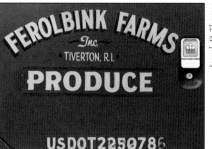

These are the priority plants on the property. All other plantings revolve around them.

The moderate climate Ferolbink Farm enjoys has its pros and cons. The season is long enough. The surrounding waterways allow for cool temperatures when the plants need it and keep frost at bay at least two weeks past inland areas. Planting begins in April and harvest stretches from early August through November, each potato variety maturing at its own rate. However, the moisture that moderates also provides a friendly environment for blight (the fungus behind the Great Irish Potato Famine). Our unpredictable New England weather is like a dog at Pete's heels. Hurricanes tear up plants, heavy rains expose the shallow-growing tubers to sunlight, turning them green, drought weakens the plants' resistance to disease and a hard frost (28°) causes the potato to be unsalable. Starch in the vegetable turns to sugar at 50°, making it unfit for frying.

These concerns are the norm in the agricultural world. For Pete Peckham, pressures from the outside complicate the internal issues he must resolve daily. Ever-changing codes, laws, tax criteria and industry standards add confusion to seemingly simple situations. Successful cooperatives, he feels, may not only save the small farmer but lend them strength. Who are the major competitors for potato chip company business? Corporate farms with acreage exceeding 6,000, each worldwide with numerous storage facilities; also highly

Ferolbink fields along the Sakonnet River, ready for planting

organized state cooperatives of independent farmers boasting 10 to 15,000 acres. Standards set by these well-financed organizations press Pete Peckham to compete on their terms. For example, if a large organization floods the grocery stores with a new bag size, retailers, knowing their shoppers like consistency, will demand that package from all their suppliers. For Pete, that could mean purchasing a $50,000 bagger. Shifting size

Land meets water at Ferolbink along Route 77

and redefining the grading has the same effect, outdating equipment used to sort and grade. "It is not unusual for these large cooperative farms to invest in a million dollar packing line to satisfy the needs of their market. We must constantly change to compete and keep our own markets."

The mild manner and no-nonsense demeanor of Pete Peckham are strong indicators that he takes all of this in stride. He also takes time for young people and he speaks with excitement about the children from Tiverton and Little Compton who visit his farm twice a year, for the spring planting and fall harvest. He believes programs like "Ag in the Classroom," which opens up the wonders of farming and the rural life to inner-city children, will advance the future of farming. Ferolbink also hires a few local teenagers each season to put in several three-hour shifts per week handpicking squash. Pete loves to have young people around, watching them work hard for the joy of it.

Potato harvest at Ferolbink

This life on the farm is a good one in the hearts and minds of its owners. The Peckhams do "get away" for a while in February, but are happy to come home and resume their rigorous dawn-to-dusk workday. They have encouraged their children to choose this life, and son Jason and nephew Tyler Young are next in line to cultivate the Ferolbink lands. Despite the long hours and the unpredictability of nature, would Pete Peckham do this all over again? "Of course."

John K. Robson

Selecting Pumpkins, Squash and Potatoes

Joseph D. Thomas

Sysco produce-buyer Manny Furtado examines the product at Ward's Berry Farm.

Not all pumpkins are good for pies! The big jack o' lanterns aren't ideal, but sugar pies are perfect. Mini pumpkins are good for decoration and also for eating. Baby boos and jack be littles, tops cut and scooped out, can be baked until tender and used to hold soup or a sweet dessert custard.

The selection of winter squash is exciting and most can be handled the same. A big gray hubbard may require a little extra effort to cook. I have vivid memories of my mother with a hammer and wedge splitting open a monster hubbard to be roasted for Thanksgiving. I hope my enjoyment was worth her efforts.

When purchasing any squash or pumpkin, make sure the skin is firm to the touch with no mushy spots or excessive wrinkling. Certain varieties are bumpy by nature, so check with the grower if you are unsure. Local summer squash is available June through September, then start looking for the winter varieties and the pumpkins.

Avoid soft wrinkling potatoes. I have a deep kitchen drawer where I store my winter squash, potatoes, garlic and onions. However, most summer squash, with the exception of pumpkins, should be kept in the refrigerator.

Potato Cakes

1 med. yellow onion, minced
2 tsp. olive oil
2 cups mashed potato
2 eggs, beaten
¼ cup plain yogurt
1 tbsp. chopped chives or
    parsley
Grated orange zest (optional)
Salt and pepper
Canola oil

OPTIONS:
Fold into the mixture:
¼ cup whole baby clams or
¼ cup corn kernels and 1 finely
    minced chili pepper or
2 tbsp. chopped cooked bacon, or
    1 tbsp. mashed roasted garlic
    and 4 minced Spanish olives

This recipe was inspired by my Grandmother Downey's codfish cakes, which are potato based. By removing the fish, she set this dish up to be very versatile.

Cook the onions in the olive oil, slowly over medium heat, until very soft and translucent. Remove from the heat and cool.

In a mixing bowl, fold the egg, yogurt, chives, zest and onions into the potato until thoroughly combined, using as few strokes as possible. Season with salt and pepper to taste. Form the mixture into 8 small patties.

Heat a sauté pan over medium heat and pour in about 2 tablespoons of canola oil. When the oil is quite hot, gently place the cakes into the pan and cook until brown on both sides. Serve warm. The cakes can be cooled and stored for a day in the refrigerator, then heated in a toaster oven.

MAKES 4 SERVINGS.

Sausage and Winter Vegetable Scramble

Here's an easy, economical casserole your family is sure to enjoy.

Prick sausage several times each with a fork and drop into boiling water. Boil for 5 minutes. Drain. When cool, cut into ¼" slices. Heat oil in a large, heavy skillet. Add sliced sausage and brown on both sides. Remove from skillet with a slotted spoon and discard all but 1 tablespoon of fat.

Briefly sauté onion in reserved fat. Stir in cabbage and potatoes. Add water or chicken stock, cover and simmer for 10–15 minutes, until potatoes are tender. Add salt and pepper to taste. Cover with sausage pieces and grated light cheddar cheese, then run under the broiler just until cheese is melted.

MAKES 4–5 SERVINGS.

Ken Haedrich, Culinary Impressions for Cabot Creamery, Cabot, VT

½ lb. sweet Italian sausage
1 tbsp. oil
1 small onion, chopped
3 cups thinly shredded cabbage
2 cups peeled potatoes, cut in ½" cubes
1 cup water or chicken stock
Salt and pepper to taste
1½ cups grated Cabot light cheddar cheese

John K. Robson

New England Clam Chowder

In a heavy stockpot, melt butter and sauté onions until softened over a medium flame. Add flour, stir in to make a roux and cook over low heat for 5-7 minutes, stirring continuously to prevent browning. Cook until you smell the cooked flour. In a separate pot, simmer the potatoes in clam juice with celery salt and poultry seasoning until tender. Add chopped clams or quahogs and simmer 1 minute. Drain liquid into roux, mixing until smooth over medium heat. Then stir potatoes, clams, chopped parsley and light cream into the roux and simmer for 5 minutes. Add salt and pepper to taste.

MAKES 10-12 CUPS.

Gregory J. Jasinski, Corporate Chef, Bittersweet Farm Restaurant and Tavern, Westport, MA

8 oz. butter or margarine
2 cups onions, diced
½ cup flour
1½ lbs. white potatoes, peeled, diced
4 cups clam juice
½ tsp. celery salt
½ tsp. poultry seasoning
1 pt. chopped quahogs or clams, fresh
2 tbsp. chopped parsley, fresh
2 cups light cream

Westport farm

John K. Robson

Country Potato Paté
with Rosemary Applesauce

1 russet potato, peeled and
    quartered
1 lb. chicken livers, rinsed and
    trimmed of fat
1 egg
¼ tsp. salt
6 turns ground black pepper
2 tsp. Noble Chardonnay
    cognac or sweet wine
2 red-skinned baking apples
    (macintosh, rome)
¼ cup water
¼ tsp. fresh rosemary leaves
Tiny pinch cinnamon
8 slices brioche or sweet bread
Softened butter

Red and white potatoes

This flavorful paté relies on potato starch rather than additional fat for its smooth texture and richness.

Preheat oven to 350°. Lightly butter or spray a 1-quart glass loaf pan. Cook the potato over medium heat in simmering water until completely tender, drain and mash it thoroughly until only small lumps remain. Chill. Place the livers, egg, wine, and seasonings in a food processor and blend until liquefied. Pour into a mixing bowl and whisk in the potato. Transfer the mixture into a glass loaf pan and set in a warm water bath. Bake until the paté is set and cooked through, about 1½ hours. Allow to cool for 15 minutes, turn out onto a plate. Wrap in film and chill. Quarter, core, and cube the apples and place in a small sauce pot with the water, rosemary and cinnamon. Cover and simmer over low heat until the apples are collapsing, approximately 8 minutes. Remove from the heat and crush any larger pieces with a masher. The applesauce should remain lumpy. Hold warm until use. Lightly butter the bread and cut in quarters on the diagonal. Line the triangles up on a cookie sheet and toast in a 450° oven for several minutes until golden.

To assemble: Slice the paté and cut each slice into wedges. Set on the toast and top with warm applesauce.

Makes 8 appetizers.

Fresh food at Ward's farmstand in Sharon

Joseph D. Thomas

Potato and Onion Tart

This tart is excellent as a main course when accompanied by fresh vegetables tossed with olive oil and salt, or served as a rich side dish.

Preheat oven to 400°. Peel the potatoes, cut two in thirds, leaving the other three whole, and set the cut spuds in a small saucepan with a pinch of salt and the garlic cloves. Cover them with cold water, bring to a boil over high heat, then lower the temperature to simmering and cook the potatoes until tender. Drain them over a bowl to retain their cooking liquid, return them to their pot and crush the potatoes and garlic with a masher. Pour in ¼ cup cooking liquid, 2 tablespoons half-and-half, butter or oil and nutmeg, then stir with a wooden spoon. Add more liquid as needed to make fluffy mashed potatoes. Season with salt and pepper to taste.

While the mashies are cooking, butter the pie dish, then thinly slice the remaining potatoes by hand or with the slicing disk of a food processor. Lay the slices on the bottom of the pie dish, overlapping the edges, then spread the onion slices over the top. Sprinkle with salt and pepper and drizzle with half-and-half until the level of liquid is even with the potatoes. Spread the mashed potatoes over the top and sprinkle with parmesan cheese. Bake for about 30 minutes until browned and bubbly. Allow the tart to sit for at least 10 minutes before slicing. Garnish each slice with chives.

MAKES ONE 9" PIE OR 6 MAIN DISHES OR 8–10 SIDE DISHES.

5 russet potatoes (about 2 lbs.)
3 cloves garlic
1 med. yellow onion, peeled and thinly sliced
1 cup half-and-half
2 tsp. unsalted butter or olive oil
Salt, black pepper
Pinch nutmeg
2 tbsp. freshly grated parmesan cheese
1 tbsp. chopped chives

John K. Robson

Greenhouse garlic at Ward's Berry Farm in Sharon

Red onions

John K. Robson

Squash Pancakes

1 cup squash purée (butternut,
    delicata, sweet dumpling)
¼ cup white cornmeal
1 tsp. salt
2 tbsp. butter, melted
1 tsp. baking powder
½ tsp. chopped fresh ginger
2 large eggs, separated
Canola oil or non-stick spray

The flavor of these pancakes is slightly sweet and very tender. They are delicious just off the heat, or cook them ahead and reheat briefly, covered, in a low oven.

Stir together the purée, cornmeal, salt, butter, baking powder and ginger, then stir in the egg yolks. In a separate bowl, beat the egg whites to a soft peak, then fold into the squash mixture in two additions.

Heat a nonstick pan or pancake skillet over medium heat until just hot. Spray with nonstick spray or oil lightly. Spoon batter into pan to make 2" cakes. Cook until the cakes dry out along the edges. Flip carefully and cook until puffed and golden. Serve alongside roasted pork or baked salmon, or serve under chicken salad for lunch.

MAKES 1 DOZEN.

Squash and gourds at Westport Fair

John K. Robson

John K. Robson

Dinner on the Grill

Paul Costa loves grilled food and bold spices, but he doesn't use a recipe. These two are for him. Eat this meal outside with fresh bread and iced tea or a cold beer.

When the grill is ready, brush the steaks lightly with oil and season with salt and pepper. Grill on both sides to desired temperature (Paul likes it rare). Brush the pepper with oil and toss on the grill. Split the squash lengthwise, brush both sides with oil and season with salt and pepper. Grill split side down until tender, then pull aside. Cook the pepper by rolling on the grill as each side gets color and blisters. Pull over to a cooler side of the grill and let steam until tender. Split the pepper and pull out the seeds. Lay the pepper sections flat and scrape off the skin. Serve with the pepper draped over the steak. Paul Costa may add a dash of hot sauce if needed.

MAKES 2 SERVINGS.

2 semi-boneless Delmonico
  steaks
1 fiery chile pepper
2 zucchini or yellow squash
Canola oil
Salt, pepper

John K. Robson

Hot chiles at Costa Farm

Grilled Zucchini Pizza

This recipe makes use of that zucchini that seems to triple in size overnight.

Brush the zucchini with the oil on its cut side and set down on a hot grill until it is marked. Brush the rounded side and flip. Spread on an even layer of sauce on the cut side of the squash and sprinkle with cheese. Cook until tender. Cover with lid if necessary.

MAKES 4 OR MORE SERVINGS.

1 gigantic zucchini, split
  lengthwise
canola oil
up to 2 cups tomato sauce
1 cup grated cheese (monterey
  jack, parmesan or
  mozzarella)

George Farm squash fields, encircled by rapidly developing house lots

Joseph D. Thomas

Summer Squash Casserole

2 lbs. yellow summer squash, sliced
2 lbs. zucchini, sliced
1 cup chopped onion
2 cans cream of mushroom soup
2 cups sour cream
2 cups shredded carrots
8 oz. pkg. herb stuffing mix
½ cup butter

A delicious addition to any meal, this recipe is a favorite, made famous by Mrs. Albert Lees.

In saucepan, cook sliced squash and chopped onion in boiling salted water for 5 minutes. Drain thoroughly. Combine soup and sour cream. Stir in carrots. Fold in squash and onion. Combine stuffing and butter. Spread three-quarters of the stuffing mix on bottom of baking dish. Spoon the vegetables over the stuffing mix. Spread remaining stuffing mix over the top. Bake at 350° for 25–30 minutes.

Makes 1½-quart casserole.

Lees Super Market, Westport, MA

John K. Robson

Summer squash

Butternut Squash Soup with Apple Cider

¼ cup canola or vegetable oil
2 onions, peeled and cut into ½" dice
3 ribs celery, chopped into ½" dice
2 carrots, peeled and sliced
2 leeks, split, rinsed and sliced
3 lbs. butternut squash, seeded, peeled and cubed into ¾" dice
2 potatoes, peeled and diced
6 cups chicken or vegetable stock
2 cups apple cider
2 cups heavy cream
Salt and pepper to taste

Squash soups are a local favorite and there are as many versions as there are soup pots. The following two recipes yield rich delicious soups, but require completely different preparations.

Heat the oil in a large soup pot over medium heat and "sweat" the onions, celery, carrots and leeks until softened. Add squash, potatoes and stock to the vegetables. Boil and simmer until all ingredients are completely cooked. Add apple cider, bring to a boil, then remove from heat. Purée soup in blender in batches until smooth and return to pot. Add cream to the soup and season with salt and pepper to taste. Serve immediately.

Makes 8 servings.

Stephen Worden, Worden's 7 Water Street Restaurant, Dartmouth, MA

Harvesting butternut squash at Ferolbink Farm

John K. Robson

Smooth Squash Soup

This soup can be made with buttercup, butternut, delicata, hubbard squash, or sugar pumpkin. Each squash has subtle differences but their texture when roasted is very similar. I roast the veggies for this soup to get a caramel richness in the flavor. The beauty of a soup like this is its flexibility. An extra pound of squash, more potatoes, fewer carrots do not hurt it. The purpose of this sort of dish is to make life easier by making use of commonly found ingredients.

1–3 lbs. butternut or another variety of squash, split lengthwise and seeded
3 carrots, peeled
2 med. yellow onions, split lengthwise, skin on
5 cloves garlic
4 sauce apples, cored, unpeeled and cut in ½" chunks
1 lb. red or white potatoes, cut in ½" slices (about 3)
2 qts. vegetable or chicken stock
Salt

Preheat oven to 400°. Place the squash cut-side down in a sprayed baking dish. Toss the carrots and onions in a little canola oil and salt. If there is room in the baking dish, lay out the carrots and set in the onions cut-side down. If not, arrange in a separate pan. Roast the vegetables until tender…the carrots and onions should be ready in 20–30 minutes, the squash may take up to an hour to be completely tender. A knife inserted in any of the vegetables should meet with no resistance.

Place the onions (peeled), carrots and roasted squash (scooped out of its skin) into a 6–8-quart soup pot. Add the garlic, apples, potatoes and stock. Add water if needed to just cover the ingredients. Bring to a boil. Lower to a simmer and cook until the potatoes are fall-apart tender. Purée the soup with a hand blender, bar blender or food processor. (It is best to cool a soup before using a bar blender. Steam builds up in the canister and makes an exploding squash bomb at start-up.) Return the soup to the pot and season with salt to taste.

Makes approximately 3 quarts.

Small pumpkins at George Farm

Butternut squash

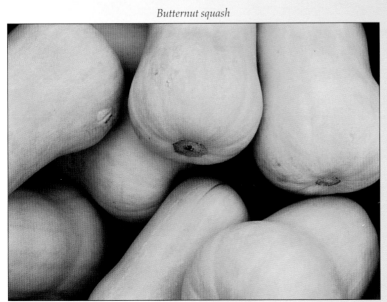

John K. Robson

Roasting Squash

The wonderful world of squash gives us so many available options to cook with, but each type needs its own special handling.

Spaghetti squash: Preheat oven to 350°. Split in half lengthwise. Scoop out seeds. Set split side down in a roasting pan in ½" of water. A 2½ lb. squash takes 30–40 minutes to cook fork-tender. Cool for 10 minutes. Scoop out and separate with a fork into spaghetti-like strands. Season with butter or oil and salt. (A microwave is another option. Cook the half-squash on high for about 4 minutes per side, turning it over once.)

Butternut, dumpling, delicata, hubbard, buttercup and acorn (winter squashes): Preheat oven to 350°. Roast cut side up on a baking sheet seasoned with salt until tender. Roast at least 30 minutes for 2½–3 lb., or until tender. Some varieties need more cooking time. Mash with butter and season with salt.

Summer squash, zucchini, crook neck, etc.: Preheat oven to 425°. Split the squash in half lengthwise, toss in a bowl with canola oil and salt. Set cut-side down on a roasting pan. Cook for about 12 minutes for squash about an inch and a half in diameter.

John K. Robson

Squash blossoms in greenhouse at Eva's Garden

Scarecrow keeps watch over pumpkin and squash fields at Ward's Berry Farm.

Joseph D. Thomas

Pumpkin Bread

Preheat oven to 350°. Combine flour, sugar, baking soda and salt in a large bowl. Make a well in the center and add the remaining ingredients. Stir well for 2 minutes. Pour into buttered loaf pans. Bake for 40–50 minutes until toothpick inserted in center comes out clean.

MAKES 3 STANDARD LOAVES.

Sue Smith, Noquochoke Orchards, Westport, MA

3½ cups flour
3 cups sugar
2 tsp. baking soda
1½ tsp. salt
4 eggs, well beaten
1 cup oil
⅔ cup cold water
1¾ cups cooked and mashed pumpkin
1 tsp. nutmeg
1 tsp. cinnamon

Baked Pumpkin Bread Pudding

Preheat oven to 350°. Butter or spray a rectangular glass or ceramic baking dish. Whisk together the eggs, sugar and pumpkin. Stream in the half-and-half, whisking constantly. Stir in the spices. Set the slices of bread into the glass pan and pour the custard over the top. Bake until puffed and set in the center, 50 minutes to 1 hour. Serve warm or cooled with cream or ice cream. Store leftovers in the refrigerator.

MAKES 9" X 13" BAKING DISH.

Butter or cooking spray
4 large eggs
½ cup sugar
1 cup pumpkin purée
2 cups half-and-half
½ tsp. cinnamon
Pinch nutmeg
8 slices sweet bread

Pumpkin Cookies

Preheat oven to 350°. Cream butter and sugars with an electric mixer until fluffy. Combine pumpkin, eggs, orange extract and vegetable oil in a separate bowl, then beat into butter and sugar mixture. Mix together dry ingredients and fold in gently in two batches. Spoon dough onto a greased cookie sheet. Bake for 20–25 minutes. Cool on a rack. Store in a canister.

MAKES 2 DOZEN.

Stephen Worden, Worden's 7 Water Street Restaurant, Dartmouth, MA

½ cup butter
½ cup sugar, granulated
½ cup brown sugar
1½ cups pumpkin, mashed or canned
2 eggs
1 tsp. orange extract or zest of orange
¼ tsp. vegetable oil
1¾ cups all-purpose flour
1 tsp. baking soda
¼ tsp. salt
1½ tsp. pumpkin pie spice

CHAPTER THREE

Corn, Beans & Tomatoes

All the inhabitants of this place are much given to agriculture, and lay up a store of Indian Corn for the winter. —Samuel Champlain, Cape Cod, 1606

The Native American diet brimmed with variety, but the three most important crops to the agriculture-based native tribes were corn, beans and squash, the "Three Sisters." All three were planted together, making use of tilled soil with a self-fertilization system. A hole was dug to plant the corn. Before pushing the soil back over the planting, a fish was dropped in on top. Then beans and squash were planted alongside the little corn hills. The beans wound their way up the growing corn stalk and the squash plants filled in the gaps between plants. Beans were harvested first, then corn, then the squash. These Native Americans demonstrated to the white settlers that their farming techniques were deliberate and polished.

Dan Minihan harvesting ripe ears at Ward's Farm

Joseph D. Thomas

Fortunately for the settlers, this agricultural education was passed along to them. From the Native Americans, the Pilgrims relearned how to choose farmland and construct tools from shell and wood. But even before they set their hoes and rakes to the soil, they were reaping the benefits of Native American technology. Their arrival in December during a particularly cruel winter meant they were without food. They discovered an emergency cache of Indian corn, which saved them from pellagra and starvation. Perhaps more than half would have died without the pillaged corn.

Betse Downey

Colonists soon learned to appreciate maize (corn) in their own kitchens, as barley, oats and wheat had not yet been planted. Cornmeal was the flour of choice. Indian samp (cornmeal mush) became the base for many traditional English dishes like custards and pan-fried cakes. The ears were also roasted whole or steamed over hot coals under a blanket of seaweed and animal skins. The English were adept in the handling of beans since most European countries had their own varieties. The peas and flat broad green beans were shelled and dried, then cooked in a large covered pot with a bit of bear fat and maple sugar—the first baked beans! Delicate green beans were harvested from healthy bushes and preferred over similar beans from Europe.

Over the years corn and beans have changed. Today there are dozens of corn varieties bred for meal, sweet-eating or high-volume feed. A grower need only choose the market and devote the land; corn swallows acreage. Beans and peas have an equally colorful evolution. Varieties are bred for eating fresh, others to dry and store for soup.

Tomatoes are a summertime treat. We wait all winter in anticipation of that first warm juicy slice. But this local favorite is a South American original, carried to Europe with Spanish explorers sometime during the 16th century. It was planted in France, Spain and Portugal, but the Italians gave the tomato its fame; Pomo d'Oro, "apple of gold," is the name they chose. The "tomata" was brought to this corner of the United States in 1802, though Thomas Jefferson had already experimented with plantings in 1781. The colonists did not appreciate its strange color and texture and rejected it as evil.

A small farmer today has a lot of competition where these crops are concerned. Big corporate farms produce an enormous volume with their concerns focused on yield and shipping. For local farmers, the market is regional and they compete primarily on the basis of quality. The people and businesses profiled in this chapter—John George of George Farm in Dartmouth and Tim McTague of Gray's Grist Mill—exemplify the important history and the uncertain future of specialty and quality-based farming.

Before we visit George Farm, this is what William Robbins says about the American tomato in *The American Food Scandal*:

> *Our tomatoes have become hard, grainy and tasteless because government researchers, serving agribusiness rather than the consumer, breed them for toughness rather than quality…developed primarily to withstand the steel fingers of mechanical harvesters. [They are] bred for mass production, without regard to flavor, picked green, and sprayed with an ethylene gas that turns them red but doesn't produce either the vitamins or the flavor of vine-ripened produce. In their cellophane-windowed cartons, they will be lined up on the counter, having been shipped across the country, while nearby farmers may have vines heavy with tomatoes that are juicy and ripe in vitamins…*

John George Farm

George Farm is located on Slocum Road in Dartmouth and boasts a generous indoor farmstand that opens with flower sales in April, with produce in June through October, then reopens in December for Christmas tree sales. The farm sells not only retail, but also through Coastal Growers Association and to several small businesses. Over a third of the farm's acreage is devoted to four types of corn. The remaining acres are chock-full of variety: tomatoes, several types of beans, an array of lettuces, kales and cabbages, cucumbers, eggplant, summer and winter squash too numerous to name, raspberries, turnips, beets, and a crazy assortment of peppers.

I met the farm's owner, John George Jr., at his business office in New Bedford, where he is president of the Union Street Bus Company. Although dressed in a pressed shirt and tie, he exuded the rugged energy and intensity I recognize as characteristic of "farmer." We discussed the family farm he runs with the help of his parents, for this farm goes back through three generations.

His grandfather, Antone George, came from Portugal and rented land on Rockdale Avenue in New Bedford. He farmed it, sold his goods in the city, saved his money and bought his first farm in Dartmouth on Old Westport Road. His father John and Uncle Joseph were born there. By 1926 the farm had grown and the family looked for new land, finally purchasing 200 acres at the current Slocum Road location. They also bought and farmed an additional 130 acres on Hathaway Road, which was sold 25 years ago. In 1956, Antone George turned the farm over to his sons John and Joseph who worked together. In 1963, they decided to split the farm business. John Jr. took over in 1989 and now oversees the 150-acre farm, with four year-round employees and 25 at peak season. His seasonal employees are almost all students.

George farmstand on Slocum Road, Dartmouth

John K. Robson

This self-professed "type A" personality built his life on farming. He doesn't play golf—farming is his relaxation. As a young man, taking care of the family lands consumed weekends, after school hours and the summertime. In the 1970s he attended Bryant College in Rhode Island and worked at a bus company while earning a degree in economics. This was a time when farming was in decline and the George family business was at a crossroads. Selling strictly wholesale was not adequate and they decided to open a retail store on the property, a path that has led to great success.

"All politics is local," said John George, Jr., quoting former House Speaker Tip O'Neil. But then, John always felt that *everything* is local. As beneficiaries of an agricultural area, maintaining and improving our quality of life rests with us, he says. This is a message he has conveyed to the community personally and through many years of public service. John served as a Dartmouth selectman for nine years, state representative for three years, and chairman of the state board of Food and Agriculture for eight years. Now retired from public service, he sees family farming again at a crossroads, and it could go either way. Drastic change is required to keep farming alive, he believes. Short of tearing down malls and reconverting the land to farms, a good place to start is with less burdensome regulations from federal and state offices and with more consistent support from local planning boards and representatives.

John George reflects the sentiments of other farmers, pointing to consumer education as the best way to ensure the market. He wishes he could tap into the motivation of shoppers and tip them off, reminding them that they really do get what they pay for. The lowest price most often equals lowest quality and comes at the expense of the small farmer. On the positive side, getting necessary information to the public helps shape their choices. Consider the issues of health and profit margin in this example: The average retail price of a doughnut is 50 cents. It costs pennies to make, has certain taste value but little to benefit health. The current price for local, in-season fresh corn on the cob is 33 cents an ear, selling at a much lower profit margin. He is delighted to see an increase in informed consumers shopping seasonally and supporting those businesses that buy local.

In the George Farm lot, a big yellow bus filled with children on a spring or autumn field trip is a common sight. Educating the young about life and work on a vegetable farm is time well spent. What is the message he would like to get out to high school or agricultural school students? "I want them to be aware of the commitment a small quality farm requires. This is a lifestyle, not a job." His great hope is that the future will allow farmers to make a decent living for their families and employees and they will have the heart and the personal wherewithal to stick with it.

What of the future of George Farm? John won't retire, just keep going until he has to stop. Who will step in? His teenage daughter is headed for college and it's too soon to see the future. In the meantime, he will continue to grow his sweet corn, experiment with new vegetables, follow and employ certain organic techniques, and ride his motorcycle very fast when he has a chance.

This interview was special for me because my family has been shopping at the George farmstand since it opened. What my mother didn't grow, or what our sizable family had exhausted in her garden, we purchased there. The taste of steamed corn on the cob, chilled green bean salad and freshly sliced tomatoes hangs sweet and heavy in my summer memories. My son Alex shops there with me now. He picks out enormous heads of lettuce, juicy yellow onions, purple shell beans, and beautiful bunches of beets. We wait together for the bag of freshly picked corn to be emptied into the bin, a sight that draws more frenzied shoppers than a sale in Filene's Basement. My hope is that my children will be able to shop at this farm with their children.

Gray's Grist Mill

"Indian Corn." This term conjures up images of chubby purple and yellow-kerneled ears strung together on the front door keeping a welcoming vigil until Thanksgiving passes. As we know, corn to the native people of this land held a much more prominent place in their lives than that of a mere ornament. In its many forms, corn was a staple of the native diet. The bulk of an annual crop was not eaten fresh, but dried and ground into meal or buried for use in the winter. Corn ground for meal must be higher in starch and lower in sugar than the summer picnic variety. I traveled to Gray's Grist Mill in Adamsville, Rhode Island, to learn more.

Gray's miller, Tim McTague, has become the local voice of the history of Indian corn. At the mill, Rhode Island white cap flint corn is ground into coarse johnnycake meal. I asked Tim about this special variety. "It is an eight-rowed white flint corn and all the kernels are the same color." This gives the meal its uniform color and texture. "It is a direct descendent of the corn grown by the local tribes for about 200 years before white people showed up in 1620."

What does it take to handle this unique crop? "It is an open pollinated corn and should be grown away from other corn varieties to prevent cross-pollination. America doesn't pay too much attention to open-pollinated corns except as gene donors to hybrids." These hybrids have become the standard for growers. New breeds will yield 150–200 bushels per acre. The Rhode Island white cap flint may get as high as 50, under the best conditions. Hybrids have been bred to dry more quickly and have greater stalk strength, making them more durable for harvesting equipment.

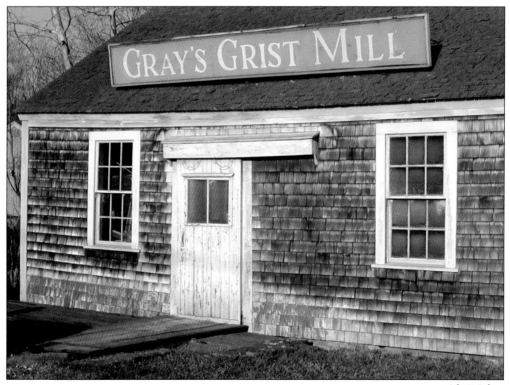

John K. Robson

The locals who grew the corn over 400 years ago chose this type for its yield and adaptability to the climate, as well as for its intended uses. However, technology has passed it by. Tim draws a comparison, "Rhode Island flint is like a Model T and the corn belt dent corn is like the 1998 Town Car. My machinery dates back to the 1950s and is about the best application of technology for the crop and for the region." Cost is another consideration. Big-crop corn sells at about eight cents per bushel. Local flint costs about 65 cents per bushel.

Johnnycake corn also requires a long growing season, 114 days from Memorial Day. After harvest, the corn is dried in a crib for up to nine months, the kernels are stripped from the ear and winnowed. Winnowing is air blowing to remove the glume, or connective membrane that holds kernel to cob. The corn is now ready for milling more than a year after planting.

All of this special care makes keeping a consistent crop more of a challenge to Tim McTague. A farmer has to consider what his acreage could potentially bring back, and Rhode Island white flint corn is obviously not the optimum crop. "The average person I buy flint corn from starts growing it for the novelty of it. By the second or third year, the thrill is fading and the grower has realized that the money isn't there. It's fun to do but it's difficult." Tim may only have the source for about six years.

To answer the question, "Why do it?" requires a visit to Gray's Mill. It's a beautiful drive on scenic backroads, no matter which direction you are coming from, and Adamsville is a charming tiny town worth visiting. The building is the original one constructed in 1675 and the enormous 15-inch thick, one-ton granite stones that grind the corn are also 300-plus-year-old originals. In a time when our computer technology is obsolete in a few months and fashions change overnight, it is overwhelming to stand in the same spot watching the same stones grind corn to meal as the first town residents of the Dartmouth Purchase did. The gears were originally powered by a water wheel in the Rocky Delano Brook. Tim's power now comes from a 1949 Farmall tractor motor, as the wheel needs reconstruction.

Besides the history of the corn and the mill, there is the johnnycake. This small, round pan-fried cake became the early settlers' best friend and main food source. (The name may have come from "journey cake," as the cakes were often wrapped and packed for long travels.) To be called a johnnycake, the batter must be made with granite-milled white flint corn, but whether the cakes are to be thick or thin depends on which Rhode Islander you ask. The preference is probably about a fifty-fifty split. Johnnycakes are more than a dietary necessity now. They are a culinary building block in our area's cultural history. There are many families whose Wednesday supper and Sunday brunch plates would have a gaping hole should their beloved Rhode Island flint corn disappear.

I suppose there is no practical reason why Tim McTague should be doing what he's doing at Gray's Mill. But it's more than just cornmeal that is going to the public. The reason Gray's still stands is the same reason we haven't filled in the Grand Canyon, disassembled Stonehenge, or mowed down the Pantheon in favor of four-plex condos. We have a lot to learn from our past, not just from the ancient past, but from yesterday. Let's take a lesson from the story of Gray's cornmeal in Adamsville, Rhode Island.

Buying and Caring for
Squash, Beans and Tomatoes

John K. Robson

Caitlin Webb harvesting at
Ward's Berry Farm

As always, avoid brown, mushy or wrinkled and overly dry veggies. Most farmstands sell fresh pickings of corn, beans and tomatoes, so rummaging through the ears of corn is probably a waste of some time. Peeling back the husk of an ear of corn is not necessary and is somewhat destructive. A fresh ear of corn has golden silk with soft, brown ends. The husk may be dry to the touch, but not shriveled. If you happen to get a worm in your corn, don't get too upset. Just get rid of him and trim off the spot he snacked on. Look for local corn July through October.

Fresh beans should hold their shape when picked up. They become flabby and lifeless as they age. Beans are available June through October. Dried beans are stored at room temperature.

Tomatoes should be heavier than they look and feel firm, but not hard. They are found in abundance from July into September. Hydroponic tomatoes are available a month or two ahead and afterward. If your farmstand is selling bags of sauce tomatoes and you have time, buy them, go home, make sauce and freeze it. Store fresh tomatoes at room temperature, but keep the one you've cut into in the refrigerator.

Inside the farmstand at Ward's

Joseph D. Thomas

Crunchy Corn Salsa

John George, Jr. laughed when I asked him about family recipes or how he cooked. I discovered he had only just purchased his first oven. You see, he eats all those yummy veggies he grows raw. His summertime breakfast consists of 3 ears of raw corn. I recommend tasting freshly picked corn raw if you have never done it. I also shave the kernels off the cob with a knife to toss in salads or mix into fresh salsa.

Shave the corn off the ear, place into a glass or stainless steel bowl. Fincly chop tomatoes and cucumber and add to corn. Toss in peppers, juice and herbs and mix well. Cover and let macerate (soak) for 15 minutes. Season to taste with salt. Serve with grilled or baked meat, chicken, fish or chips.

MAKES ABOUT 2 CUPS.

John George, Jr., George Farm, Dartmouth, MA

3 ears fresh corn, uncooked
3 fresh roma tomatoes
1 cucumber, split lengthwise and seeds scooped out
1–4 jalapeño peppers, minced (degree of heat is up to you!)
1 tbsp. lime juice
1 tsp. chopped fresh cilantro
1 tsp. chopped fresh parsley
Salt

John K. Robson

A smile and a handful from Dan Minihan at Ward's Farm

Chilled Corn Soup with Chiles

In a 2-quart pot, heat the oil over medium heat. Cook the chiles and onions until softened. Add the water and corn, bring to a boil. Add cumin and simmer for 15 minutes. Cool slightly. Purée three-quarters in a blender, then stir back into the rest of the soup. Add the cream and basil. Reheat and season to taste with salt and pepper.

MAKES 3 QUARTS.

Paul Sussman, Chef, Daddy O's and Macundo, Cambridge, MA

2 tbsp. olive oil
2 mild chiles (like anaheims)
1 hot chile (jalapeño)
1½ cups sliced onions
1 qt. water
6 ears corn, kernels sliced off the cob
1 tbsp. ground cumin
1 cup heavy cream
¼ cup basil leaves, thinly sliced
Salt and pepper

Westport corn harvest, Horseneck Road

John K. Robson

Johnnycakes

THIN JOHNNYCAKES:
2 cups johnnycake meal
½ tsp. salt
¾ cup cold water
1½ cups milk

THICK JOHNNYCAKES:
2 cups johnnycake meal
1 tsp. salt
2 cups boiling water
¼ cup milk

There are two distinct varieties. Both are delicious and excellent for break-fast or as a side for supper. Serve the cakes with syrup or fruit preserves for breakfast. Roasted turkey and ham over tender, buttered johnnycakes with a rich gravy or cranberry relish makes a hearty, cold-weather meal.

THIN JOHNNYCAKES:

Combine meal, salt and water. Stir in milk. Fry 3" cakes on a well-oiled skillet over medium-high flame until the edges are brown, then flip.

THICK JOHNNYCAKES:

Mix meal, salt and boiling water. Let stand 5 minutes. Stir in milk. Fry 1½" cakes on a well-oiled skillet over medium-high flame until the edges are brown, then flip.

MAKES ABOUT 1 DOZEN.

Gray's Grist Mill, Adamsville, RI

John K. Robson

Tim McTague shucks 8-row white cap flint corn at Gray's Grist Mill.

Indian Pudding

2¼ cups milk
4 tbsp. butter
½ cup johnnycake meal
2 lightly beaten eggs
½ cup molasses
1½ tsp. salt
1½ tsp. ginger

A very simple recipe that keeps the traditional flavors intact.

Scald 1¼ cups milk. Stir in butter, meal, eggs, molasses, salt and ginger. Pour into 1½-quart buttered casserole. Let stand 5 minutes. Pour 1 cup milk over the top. Bake at 300° for 1½ hours.

MAKES 4–6 SERVINGS.

Gray's Grist Mill, Adamsville, RI

Geese take time to view the corn fields at Ferolbink Farm in Tiverton.

John K. Robson

Savory Corn Muffins

This is a great way to use up the steamed or grilled corn left over from last night's dinner. If fresh corn is out of season, you can use thawed frozen corn as a substitute.

Lightly oil a muffin tin. In a large bowl, combine the first 9 ingredients and stir to blend. In a smaller bowl, beat the egg and add the buttermilk and oil. Fold the liquid ingredients into the dry ingredients just enough to blend. The mixture will look a bit lumpy and uneven.

Spoon the batter into the muffin tins. Bake for 16–20 minutes, depending upon your oven, or until a toothpick inserted into the center of the muffin comes out clean. Cool on a rack.

MAKES 12 MUFFINS.

Susan Kavanaugh White, Chef, Lees Super Market, Westport, MA

1 cup cornmeal
1 cup unbleached flour
1 cup sharp cheddar cheese, grated
1 cup corn kernels
½ cup thinly sliced scallions
3 strips crispy bacon, crumbled
1 jalapeño pepper, seeded, veins removed and finely minced
2 tsp. baking powder
½ tsp. baking soda
1 egg
1 cup buttermilk
¼ cup canola or vegetable oil

Micro-Steamed Corn

My mother introduced me to this fast and easy way to cook an ear of corn. Peel the outer husk down off the cob, leaving the final layer of light green husk. Snap off the long bottom stalk and cook on high in the microwave for about 3 minutes. Remove and let stand covered for another 2 minutes. The corn can be eaten as is or shaved off the cob.

Noquochoke Orchards

John K. Robson

Green Beans and Red Onion Salad

FOR THE SALAD:
1 lb. fresh beans
1 med. red onion, thick sliced
  (about a cup)
2 tsp. chopped fresh tarragon
Salt

FOR THE DRESSING:
½ cup white or cider vinegar
1 tbsp. granulated sugar
2 tbsp. canola oil

John K. Robson

FOR THE SALAD:
Snip the ends off freshly picked beans. Bring water to a boil. Drop the beans into the water and cook until bright green and tender, but not mushy (about 8 minutes). Drain, then plunge into ice water and drain again. Store in the refrigerator.

FOR THE DRESSING:
Combine the vinegar, sugar and oil. In a large bowl, toss together the beans, onion and tarragon. Toss in enough dressing to coat. Season with salt to taste. Serve chilled.

MAKES 4 SERVINGS.

Boston Baked Beans

½ lb. great northern white
  beans
4 slices bacon
1 onion, finely minced
3 cloves garlic, peeled
1 tbsp. mustard, preferably a
  rich spicy variety
¼ cup molasses
¼ cup maple syrup
Water

An original version of this recipe contained only beans, water, rendered bear or fowl fat and pepper. This recipe reflects the sweeter palate of the early settler and is what we are familiar with today.

Cover the beans with water in a large pot and bring to a boil over high heat. Lower the heat to medium and allow the beans to simmer for 20 minutes. Drain the beans in a colander, then transfer them to a large casserole. Toss the remaining ingredients with the beans, then cover the beans twice their volume with water. Bake in a 300° oven for 4-6 hours, or until tender. Check the water level of the beans as they cook and do not allow them to dry out. Add more water if necessary. Season with salt and pepper to taste.

MAKES 4–6 SERVINGS.

Ferolbink Farm, Tiverton

Joseph D. Thomas

Pasta Primavera

Fresh peas and beans give this simple pasta bright flavor and color.

Bring a large pot of lightly salted water to a boil. Blanch the peas and beans separately in the water, retrieving them with a hand strainer or slotted spoon when bright green and tender. Plunge them into ice water and drain, then hold chilled. Bring the water back to a boil and drop in the pasta.

In a large skillet, heat the canola oil over medium-high heat until hot and stir in the garlic and mushrooms. When the aroma of garlic reaches your nose, add the yellow squash and sauté until it becomes translucent around the edges. Toss in the red pepper and cook briefly. Toss in the spring onions, peas, beans and olive oil and heat thoroughly. Remove from the heat. Drain the pasta when completely cooked, transfer to a large serving bowl, and toss with the cooked veggies, cheeses and herbs. Season to taste with salt and pepper.

MAKES 4–6 SERVINGS.

1 lb. pasta of substance (penne, rigatoni, fusilli, shells)
½ cup fresh peas
1 handful string beans, ends trimmed
¼ cup canola oil
2 plump cloves garlic, minced
¼ lb. mushrooms, thinly sliced
1 yellow squash, cut in ¾" dice
1 red pepper, thinly sliced
4 spring onions (scallions), trimmed and thinly sliced
¼ cup extra virgin olive oil
¼ cup fresh basil and flat leaf parsley leaves, cleaned and packed
¼ cup freshly grated cheese (mozzarella, parmesan)
¼ cup ricotta cheese, or cottage cheese puréed smooth in a food processor
Salt and pepper

Cranberry Brown Bread

This traditional accompaniment to the early settlers, white cap flint corn "Boston Baked Beans" has been dressed up with cranberries and raspberries. The coffee can cookware and stove-top steaming method are replaced with a more practical method.

Preheat oven to 300°. In a mixing bowl combine the dry ingredients. Stir the buttermilk into the molasses in a separate bowl. Using a spoon, stir the buttermilk mixture into the dry ingredients. Fold the fruit in gently. Pour into a buttered or sprayed 9" cake pan or loaf pan and set the pan into a deep roasting pan. Pour boiling water into the roasting pan until it reaches halfway up the sides of the cake pan. Cover with foil and slide into the oven. Steam for 2 hours until fully set. Allow to sit for at least 15 minutes before slicing. Serve warm and buttered, or toast the chilled leftovers for breakfast.

MAKES ONE 9" CAKE PAN.

⅓ cup rye flour
⅔ cup whole wheat flour
½ cup yellow cornmeal
1 tsp. baking soda
½ tsp. salt
Pinch nutmeg
1 cup buttermilk (or 7 oz. milk with 1 oz. lemon juice or cider vinegar)
⅓ cup molasses
½ cup sweetened dried cranberries
½ cup fresh raspberries (optional)

Simple Tomato Sauce

1 tbsp. canola oil
3 cloves garlic, sliced
1 med. yellow onion, sliced
2 tsp. sugar
3 cups chopped tomatoes
¼ cup basil leaves
2 tbsp. olive oil, regular or extra virgin
Salt

Tomato plants at George Farm

John K. Robson

As a youth, my husband Paul lived in Italy. In his 20s, he returned to study with famed Chef Giuliano Bugiali. He wooed me with his creamy cappuccinos, spaghetti vongole (with clams) and his tasty tomato sauce. I have since used two methods to prepare it.

TRADITIONAL METHOD:
Heat the canola oil in a 1½-quart pan over medium flame. Toss in the garlic and onion and sweat until slightly softened. Sprinkle in the sugar and stir, then add the tomatoes and basil. Simmer for about 15 minutes until everything is tender. Stir in the olive oil. Season with salt and add additional sugar if needed. Purée in a blender, food processor, or with an immersion blender.

THE "I'M HOME LATE" METHOD:
Simmer all the ingredients together, except the salt and oil over a medium flame until the onions are tender. Season and purée in a similar fashion.

Sautéed mushrooms or zucchini and browned ground beef or pork can be easily stirred into the sauce. Toss warm sauce over pasta.

MAKES 3 CUPS.

Tomato Bread

1 fresh crusty French or Italian baguette, split lengthwise
2 juicy, very ripe tomatoes, split in half across the center
Olive oil
Salt

Plum tomatoes at Eva's Garden

John K. Robson

My brother-in-law Gus is from Spain. Though he is a dedicated pediatric cardiologist and practices in Florida, his passion is for his home country and its cuisine. He shared this simple recipe with me and I love it as an appetizer or alongside summertime grilled meals.

Preheat the oven to 475°, or prepare the grill. Set out the two sides of the bread cut-side up. Hold the tomatoes, one at a time over the bread and squeeze gently, then rub the tomato into the bread (kids love to do this part!) until both tomatoes are used. Drizzle well with olive oil and sprinkle lightly with salt. Place on a cookie sheet and toast in the oven until golden, or place cut-side down over medium coals to toast and color, being careful not to burn. Serve immediately.

MAKES 4–6 SERVINGS.

Tomato Breakfast Sandwiches

When tomatoes are in season, I cannot resist having them at almost every meal. Here are some simple suggestions for fast, healthy breakfast sandwiches.

Jim Ward sorts ripe tomatoes at Ward's Berry Farm.

1. 1 untoasted fresh or toasted frozen bagel
   Cream cheese
   Several basil or fresh parsley leaves
   1 large thick slice or several small slices tomato
   Black pepper

2. 1 toasted English muffin
   1 egg, scrambled
   Sliced tomatoes
   1 teaspoon chopped scallions
   Black pepper

3. 1 untoasted fresh or toasted frozen bagel
   2 slices mozzarella cheese
   Sliced tomatoes
   Balsamic vinegar (drizzle over tomatoes before assembling sandwiches)
   Several basil leaves

4. 2 slices chewy Italian bread
   Balsamic vinegar
   Extra virgin olive oil
   Tomato slices
   Salt and pepper

At the Westport Fair

CHAPTER FOUR

Apples and Peaches

*The peaches here leave behind a warm, rich and delicious taste,
that I can only liken in its effects to that which you call the bouquet of
a glass of Romanee.* —James Fenimore Cooper

The New World offered the settlers an exciting new array of culinary treasures. However, they did not abandon those things they had grown to love. Peaches and apples were two fruits not indigenous to the colonies. Peach trees were brought by Spanish explorers in the 16th century. The Native Americans fell in love with them. William Penn arrived in the Susquehanna area one hundred years later to find them already a most popular crop in the eastern Native American communities.

Acushnet apples

John K. Robson

Dozens of peach varieties are well-suited to our climate and we enjoy their fruit here by mid-to-late summer. Diane and Ernie Ventura, proprietors of the 200-year-old family farm, Ashley's Peaches, say their area of the Long Plain in Acushnet is the most northerly New England site that a peach can be grown properly. The circulating air keeps frost from settling on delicate blossoms early in the season.

Buy your fresh peaches at a local orchard that offers real tree-ripened fruit. Such peaches must be eaten or cooked within a few days of purchase. Eat at least one upon arriving home. (Eating a sun-warm, ripe peach while driving could be dangerous as eyes may roll back into your head, or juice dripping into your lap will distract.) Proper peach devotees have been known to travel over an hour several times each week on the slim chance that Ashley's in Acushnet or Westport's Noquochoke Orchards will have some left. Come with me and we'll peel away the history of Noquochoke Orchards with overseers George and Sue Smith who farm their precious peaches and their pride and joy—apples.

Apples were brought over from England by the colonists within ten years of the arrival of the first settlers. The trees adapted to the soils and climate beautifully, becoming a healthy offspring in the early farming families. Plymouth Colony Governor John Endicott purchased 200 acres of land for 500 three-year-old apple trees in 1649. Dartmouth's first representative at General Court in Plymouth, 1665, owned 3,200 acres of land (now Padanaram) that was home to a beautiful apple orchard. By 1741, the colonies were exporting the cherished fruit to the West Indies.

Early American hero Johnny Appleseed (John Chapman) was born in Massachusetts in the town of Leominster, September 26, 1774. His personal mission was to spread the fruit over as much of the country as he possibly could. Despite his seed-tossing reputation, Johnny's methods were far more organized. He carefully planted seedlings in specially selected nurseries, making his way down the east coast, then heading west. Johnny Appleseed continued his life's work until his death in March of 1845. He had gotten as far as Fort Wayne, Indiana.

The Wampanoags as well as other native people also embraced the apple and incorporated it easily into their cooking, stuffing it into roasting birds and drying it for off-season sustenance. The apple has established itself as a mainstay of this country's cooking. "As American as Apple Pie" says it all. Every corner and pocket of America has embraced it as a preferred fruit in pies, cakes, breads, sauces, stuffings and cobblers.

Macintosh and wealthy apples grow on this single tree at Noquochoke Orchards in Westport.

John K. Robson

Noquochoke Orchards

Drift Road in Westport winds along the Westport River all the way up the east branch to Head of Westport. It is a most glorious drive anytime, but especially deep in summer when the sea air mixes with the heady aroma of cut grass and fertilizer, and a breeze blows steadily throughout the afternoon. The roadsides are a postcard of old stone walls, refurbished beach and farmhouses and generous stretches of farmland. About two miles north from the Hix Bridge sits a freshly painted farmstand on the left, just opposite the large white farmhouse of Noquochoke Orchards.

The land on which Noquochoke sits has been farmed since the mid 1800s. Scottish immigrants George and Marianne Smith purchased the 100-acre orchard from Captain William Ball in 1899. Their son Alex and his wife Edale took over the farm after his parents passed away. Edale managed the orchard for 37 years with her five children: Doris, Bud, Herb, Carolyn, and George after her husband's death in 1947. In the late 1950s, the state took 20 acres by eminent domain for the construction of Route 88. The children took over and incorporated it in 1984. Today George and his wife Sue manage the orchard with their four children. Their four grandchildren love life on the farm, especially the tractors and the animals.

Orchards require an enormous amount of attention year-round: pruning in winter, pest prevention and pollination in the spring, diligent evaluation and thinning of fruit through the summer, and harvest from summer through fall. The care that goes into managing even one type of tree is awesome, but George Smith oversees the well-being of an enormous variety of trees and crops on his 80 acres. The orchard itself is home to 95 varieties of

Annie Smith at the Noquochoke farmstand

John K. Robson

apples, 16 varieties of peaches, nine pear varieties, four kinds of plums, apricots and quince. Why so many kinds of apples? "The different varieties are to keep producing a full season," he explains. There is a careful balance of early-to-late ripening with a mix of eating and cooking types to suit the diverse tastes of their buyers, including the heirloom varieties some of us prefer. Names like Rhode Island greening, winesaps, baldwins and northern spy are not as common in the grocery store as gala, fuji and golden delicious, but Noquochoke Orchards has them all.

Additional crops of strawberries, elderberries, sweet corn, squash, tomatoes and Westport macombers fill the remaining acres. Their farmstand, built in 1926, opens its doors to weekend and holiday business when the produce says it's time (no later than the beginning of August) and remains open through Thanksgiving. Weekday shoppers are encouraged to pull in the driveway. Sue will greet them and escort them to the barn to sift through the barrels and baskets of the daily harvest. The Smiths enjoy the retail side of the business, catching up with neighbors, encouraging a friend to sample an experimental peach and meeting summer visitors. George is not limited, however, to his retail outlets. His fruits and vegetables are sold through Coastal Growers Association, and he sells independently at farmers' markets, restaurants and other farmstands.

Noquochoke Orchards, like most small family farms, deals with the pressures of ever-shifting government regulations by complying but staying involved to work for change. In February 1989, George was cofounder and first vice president of the Westport Farmers Association (WFA), which was begun to help local farmers address problems. The Smiths handle their bounty with meticulous care, washing apples going into the press for the freshest cider I have ever tasted. They use their own bees for pollination. (A longtime farmer

George Smith selects ripening delicious apples at Noquochoke.

John K. Robson

and friend, Clark Chase, keeps the bees and sells their rich, dark unprocessed honey under the Zodiac label.) Promoting safe and efficient farming techniques is a priority for their own crops as well as for their area. The orchard is associated with the integrated pest management program through the University of Massachusetts in Amherst. Noquochoke Orchards is the host location for IPM training seminars every June. IPM has provided them with invaluable tools to help them cut back on pesticides, herbicides and fungicides through alternative means. Brightly colored squares around the base of their trees emit a chemical scent and act as traps for bugs that threaten to invade the orchard. Nature's own hawks and turkey buzzards frighten away black birds, and bright red sticky, apple-shaped balls attract harmful insects that tell George another spray is needed.

For the Smiths, educating themselves to effect change is not enough. They offer tours for schoolchildren and the elderly, free of charge, September through October. My son's kindergarten class scheduled a tour, so I was quick to sign up as a chaperone. The children were greeted by "Grandma Sue" on the bus and given the ground rules: "When I hold up my hand, it's time to stop and listen. Stay in the group away from the tractors, and there is NO RUNNING! " Those wiggly bundles responded respectfully and followed the leader to the orchard. The tour included a stop at Bug Hollow, where we were introduced to helpful and harmful bugs and we played a leaf identification game. We looked inside a hollow 130-year-old Rhode Island greening tree to witness how a tree feeds (from the outside), and during our walk down to the meadow that leads to the river we were told that "noquochoke" is the local Native American word meaning "east branch."

Noquochoke customer selects her own cortland apples.

Our reward at the end of the tour was a juicy apple, fresh cider and crackers with honey and crabapple jam. The children filed noisily into the bus, discussing bugs, the "picking tractor," and the giant hawks flying overhead that keep hungry crows away. As the bus pulled away, I stood, watching and hoping that this visit would remain with them, change them, help mold them. I am thrilled and comforted when my son asks about our next trip to Grandma Sue's.

John K. Robson

This poem was written by the Smiths to celebrate the living legacy of Noquochoke Orchards:

At the turn of the century in Aberdeen
A shepherd with sheep on a hill so green
Looked across the highland, lochs and North Sea
And said, "America is where we should be!"
So George with Marianne, a bonnie lass
Shipped out on a boat, and it wasn't first class!
With their kilts, tams, pipes, and shepherd's crook,
Landed in Canada, but after a look,
Migrated to Westport, a sea and farm town,
And there they both really settled down.
They worked the land near the river banks,
and on Sunday to the Lord gave thanks.
After hard work with the cows and chickens,
Also two children, "cute as the dickens!"
The land was cleared and the apple trees planted.
Now, a lot of their prayers were granted.
From their two living children came many more;
Alex's family is on laddie four!
How proud Grandpa George would be
If he had only lived to see,
Three George's working side by side,
But unfortunately, he had died.
So today, Grandpa George's farm and land
Is a legacy he left, and it sure is grand!

John K. Robson

Delicious apples, Noquochoke

Flying Cloud Orchards, Acushnet

John K. Robson

Selecting Apples and Peaches

John K. Robson

Yellow delicious apples at Noquochoke Orchards, Westport

A good apple should be firm and smell sweet. Depending on variety, local apples are ready from July through October.

A tree-ripened peach has to be eaten within a day or two. A firm peach should be stored at room temperature until it is soft enough to use. Both fruits can be held in a basket out of direct sun, but should be chilled if they are softening and won't be used right away. Wash the fruit thoroughly but gently under running water to avoid bruising.

Apple Skillet Pancake

2 firm cooking apples, peeled, cored and sliced
2 tbsp. sugar
2½ tbsp. Cabot butter
3 eggs
½ cup milk
⅓ cup cornmeal
¼ cup flour
¼ tsp. salt
1 cup grated Cabot light cheddar cheese

A special treat for a weekend family breakfast.

Preheat oven to 425°. Toss apples with sugar. Reserve. Melt the butter in a 9" or 10" cast-iron skillet and remove from heat. Beat eggs and milk in a bowl with 1 tablespoon of the melted butter. Combine cornmeal, flour and salt in a separate bowl and whisk in egg/milk mixture until smooth. Put skillet back on heat and sauté the apples in the remaining butter. After 2 or 3 minutes, before they get mushy, spread the apples evenly in the pan and gently pour on the batter. Put skillet in oven and bake for 15–20 minutes, until firm and puffy. Loosen with a spatula and invert onto an ovenproof platter. Sprinkle with grated light cheddar cheese and return to oven to melt.

MAKES 6 SERVINGS.

Cabot Creamery, Cabot, VT

Picking macoun apples at Braley Farm, Acushnet

John K. Robson

Caramel Apple Spoon Bread

This very rich and delicious spoon bread can be served with brunch or as a dessert with vanilla ice cream.

FOR THE APPLES:

Pour the sugar in the bottom of a deep-sided sauté pan and moisten with water until it is the consistency of a thick paste. Set the pan over a medium heat and cook until it liquefies, then begins to turn golden. Do not stir or disturb until sugar starts to color. When it is light golden in color, add the apples and cook until tender, about 10 minutes. Butter a 2-quart soufflé dish and set the apples into the bottom of the dish and drizzle a little caramel over them.

FOR THE BREAD:

Preheat oven to 375°. In a saucepan, heat the cream, butter, honey and salt until hot and the butter has melted. Stir in the cornmeal and cook over a low flame, stirring continuously, until thickened. Transfer the cornmeal mush to a large mixing bowl and allow to cool for several minutes, stirring occasionally. Stir in the baking powder, pepper, cinnamon and ginger, then add the egg yolks and stir until combined thoroughly. In a separate bowl, beat the egg whites briskly until soft peaks form, then fold into the spoon bread base in two additions using large, gentle strokes with a rubber spatula. Transfer to the prepared soufflé dish and bake until golden brown and puffed through the center, about 30-35 minutes. Allow the bread to cool for 10 minutes before serving. It can be spooned from the dish or turned out on a serving plate.

MAKES 1–1½-QUART SOUFFLÉ DISH.

1 cup granulated sugar
Water
2 firm apples such as granny smith, peeled, halved, cored and thinly sliced
2 cups half-and-half
3 tbsp. unsalted butter
2 tsp. honey
½ tsp. salt
1 cup johnnycake or cornmeal
5 eggs, separated
1 tsp. baking powder
6 turns freshly ground black pepper
¼ tsp. cinnamon
¼ tsp. chopped fresh or ground ginger
Pinch nutmeg

Old cider press

Flying Cloud Orchards, Acushnet

John K. Robson

Apple Pound Cake

2 tsp. cinnamon
2 cups plus 5 tsp. sugar
3 or 4 apples, peeled and sliced
4 eggs
1 cup oil
½ cup orange juice
2½ tsp. vanilla
3 cups flour
3 tsp. baking powder

Preheat oven to 350°. Grease and flour a tube pan. Mix cinnamon and the 5 teaspoons sugar. Blend together with apples and put to one side. Combine eggs, oil, orange juice and vanilla. Mix together flour, sugar and baking powder in a separate bowl, then make a well in the center. Pour in the egg mixture. Mix well. In tube pan, starting with the batter, alternate with apple mixture. Bake 1¼ hours.

MAKES 1 TUBE PAN.

Sue Smith, Noquochoke Orchards, Westport, MA

Apple Crisp

8 apples, sliced and peeled
1 tsp. cinnamon
½ cup water

TOPPING:
1 cup light brown sugar, packed
¼ cup flour
7 tbsp. butter

Preheat oven to 375°. Spread apples, cinnamon and water on bottom of a buttered casserole or baking dish. Work together remaining ingredients until crumbly. Spread over apple mixture in baking dish. Bake for 30 minutes. Serve warm with ice cream or whipped cream.

MAKES ONE 9" X 13" BAKING DISH.

Sue Smith, Noquochoke Orchards, Westport, MA

Cortlands at Noquochoke Orchards

John K. Robson

Chocolate Applesauce Cake

Preheat oven to 350°. Grease and flour a loaf pan. Cream butter and sugar. Add soda to applesauce and then add to mixture. Mix in flour and spices and beat well. Fold in nuts and raisins. Bake 50–60 minutes, until inserted toothpick comes out dry.

MAKES 3 STANDARD LOAVES.

Sue Smith, Noquochoke Orchards, Westport, MA

½ cup butter, softened
1 cup sugar
1½ cups applesauce
1½ tsp. baking soda
2 cups sifted flour
½ tsp. cinnamon
½ tsp. cloves
½ tsp. nutmeg
½ tsp. allspice
2 tbsp. cocoa
¼ tsp. salt
Nuts and raisins (optional) up to
   ¾ cup each

Apple-Peach Bread

Preheat oven to 325°. Combine sugar and oil. Beat in egg, milk and vanilla. Mix well. Sift flour and baking soda into the egg mixture and beat for 2 minutes. Fold in apples, peaches and nuts. Pour into 2 greased and floured loaf pans. Bake for 40–45 minutes (bananas or pears may be substituted for peaches).

MAKES 2 STANDARD LOAVES.

Sue Smith, Noquochoke Orchards, Westport, MA

1½ cups brown sugar, packed
⅔ cup oil
1 egg
1 cup sour milk (1 tbsp. vinegar
   added to 1 cup milk)
1 tsp. vanilla
2½ cups flour
1 tsp. baking soda
1 cup diced peaches
½ cup chopped nuts
1 cup diced apples

Peaches at Ward Berry Farm

Joseph D. Thomas

Dad's Apple Cake

1½ cups sugar
2 eggs
2 tsp. vanilla
⅔ cup canola or vegetable oil
2 cups flour
½ tsp. salt
1 tsp. baking soda
½ tsp. cinnamon
2 med. apples, peeled, cored
   and sliced
1 cup nuts, finely chopped

My father-in-law is a fabulous cook. I am often the beneficiary of such treasured recipes as this one. This cake is rich and moist, so a thin slice is sufficient.

Preheat oven to 350°. In a large bowl cream sugar and eggs. Add vanilla and oil and mix. Add flour, salt, baking soda and mix until batter is stiff but still moist. Mix cinnamon with apples and stir into batter. Spray a tube or bundt pan with non-stick spray. Sprinkle pan with finely chopped nuts, then add batter. Bake for about 50–60 minutes until tester inserted near center comes out clean. Cool in pan for about 10 minutes. Loosen cake from sides and turn out on rack and cool completely. Sprinkle with powdered sugar. Serve slightly warm with whipped cream or ice cream.

MAKES 1 TUBE OR BUNDT PAN.

Ronald Romaniello, Dartmouth, MA

Crab apple tree, Noquochoke Orchards

John K. Robson

Veal Medallions with Native Peaches and Gorgonzola Cheese

Buttered asparagus and bread will finish this elegant dish.

Dust veal with flour, one at a time, shaking off excess. Sauté veal in 1 tbsp. of butter over medium-high heat until lightly browned. Remove and transfer to a serving platter. Add sliced peaches to the pan and cook 3–5 minutes, or until softened. Add stock and wine. Bring to slow boil and reduce volume by half. Add cheese and cream, and continue to cook until the sauce thickens slightly. Stir in remaining butter. Serve sauce over veal medallions.

MAKES 2 SERVINGS.

Stephen Worden, Worden's 7 Water Street Restaurant, Dartmouth, MA

1 lb. veal medallions
1 cup flour
3 tbsp. unsalted butter
2 native peaches, seeded and
  sliced
¼ cup veal or chicken stock
¼ cup white wine
3 tbsp. gorgonzola cheese
¼ cup heavy cream

Flambé of Pears and Apples with Autumn Spices

Heat a skillet over a medium-high flame, add butter. Toss in the fruit when the butter stops foaming. Sauté until tender. Add brandy (flambé if possible). Add spices and remove from heat. Serve over vanilla ice cream.

MAKES 4 SERVINGS.

Stephen Worden, Worden's 7 Water Street Restaurant, Dartmouth, MA

1 tbsp. unsalted butter
2 apples, peeled, cored and
  sliced
2 pears, peeled, cored and sliced
¼ cup brandy or apple jack
  liqueur
¼ tsp. cinnamon
¼ tsp. cardamom
¼ tsp. nutmeg
¼ tsp. ginger
Pinch ground cloves

Bartlett pears at Noquochoke

John K. Robson

Peach Crust

3–4 roasted peaches, peeled,
  pitted and sliced
8 oz. cream cheese, softened
2 sheets frozen puff pastry
Granulated sugar

Ashley Farm peaches, Acushnet

When peaches are their ripest, I do not cook with them that much. In our house, we are perfectly content to slurp on them hanging over the railing of the deck. I will, for a dessert, roast them whole and serve them with cream and cookies. This "crust" came together because I needed a dessert quickly, and all I had on hand was cream cheese, puff pastry and roasted peaches.

TO ROAST THE PEACHES:
Preheat the oven to 450°. Set peaches several inches apart, upside down, on a rack set in a roasting pan. Roast for at least 20 minutes. The fruit may take up to an hour, depending on size and ripeness. They are completely cooked when they give easily when gently squeezed on the sides and juice has started to bubble out from the stem end. Remove them from the oven and transfer them to a glass or ceramic dish to cool. Store wrapped tightly in the refrigerator.

FOR THE "CRUST":
Preheat the oven to 425°. To peel the peaches, hold them gingerly over a bowl while pulling the skin off with a small sharp knife. If the fruit is properly cooked, the skin will peel right off. Split the peach in half, top to bottom, to remove the pit. The juice from the peach should be dripping into the bowl. Slice the halves on a clean cutting board, then lift them gently and lay them out flat onto a plate. The juice on the board should be scraped with a rubber spatula into the juice bowl.

In another bowl, beat the cream cheese with a wooden spoon until smooth, then stir in 2 tablespoons of the peach juice.

Roll out the puff pastry in granulated sugar to about ⅛" thickness. Slide it onto a cookie sheet lined with parchment or sprayed with non-stick spray.

Spread an even layer of cream cheese mixture over the pastry, then arrange the peaches on top. Bake until the pastry is golden brown on the bottom and the cream cheese has puffed slightly, about 12–15 minutes. Allow to cool on the pan for several minutes. Slice into squares and serve. Fresh mint leaves are a tasty garnish.

To use leftover peach juice, stir into yogurt, seltzer water, or your morning glass of juice.

MAKES 6–8 SERVINGS.

Fresh Peach Smoothie

A good "smoothie" can be made with almost any fruit, but fresh peach, when it's a bit too overripe to eat whole, is a favorite. I love to sip this for breakfast, lunch or a snack.

Put everything in the blender and whip on high until smooth, creamy and foamy. A "smoothie" can be stored in the refrigerator covered, but the color will darken as it sits and will not be as foamy.

MAKES 2 LARGE SERVINGS.

1 very ripe, pitted peach, peeled is optional
1 medium to very ripe (but not gooey) banana, peeled
1 cup unflavored or vanilla yogurt (any fat level)
1½ cups milk (any fat level)
1 tbsp. honey
¼ cup crushed ice

Peaches and Wine

I am someone who truly appreciates good wine of any price, variety or country of origin, yet I have never developed a taste for wine coolers. However, my mother-in-law Barbara presented me with a glass of this wonderful beverage on a very hot July afternoon. It was light, refreshing, fruity and slightly sweet. She told me she learned to make it in Italy. Like any recipe of this sort, you use what you have in the house and the taste is never identical. These quantities are approximate, but should point in the right direction.

Slightly crush the peaches and slide into a nice glass carafe or decanter. Pour the wine over and chill. It is best if it sits overnight. Serve chilled.

MAKES 4–5 CUPS.

2 cups very ripe peaches, pitted and sliced
4 cups dry white wine (riesling, gewurztraminer, sauvignon or fumé blanc, or any white of your choice)

Peach baskets for sale at Ward's farmstand

John K. Robson

CHAPTER FIVE

Berries and More Berries

This main is the goodliest continent that we ever saw… for it is
replenished with fair fields…also meadows hedged in with stately groves.
—M. John Brereton, *Gosnold's Discoveries in the North Parts of Virginia*

nglish explorer Bartholomew Gosnold and his crew skimmed the shores of Buzzards Bay and the islands, then called North Virginia, in 1602 on a fact-finding mission. They kept careful accounts of the terrain, especially the available natural resources of foodstuffs. Much was written about the dizzying array of berries: strawberries (larger than those in England), gooseberries, raspberries, huckleberries, blackberries and blueberries; the latter closely resembled the English bilberry.

John K. Robson

John K. Robson

Blueberries, along with their flavorful relatives, were well woven into the diet of the native tribes. They were eaten fresh, but were also dried and used whole, or ground into flour to thicken stews, or baked into simple cakes. Early settlers arrived with their own traditional recipes and the berries of their new home were easy replacements for the varieties left behind.

So many kinds of berries thrive in the acidic, sandy soil of New England. The "craneberry," or cranberry as it has come to be known, is the ruby in the crown of our culinary history.

Cranberries are native to North America and well-suited to our climate. Their particular brand of acidity is best developed in this environment of long, cool summers. The Native Americans ate the fruit fresh or dried and brewed in teas, and as a major ingredient of pemmican. Pemmican was a hard "survival cake" of dried meat, fat and cranberries beaten together into a sausage, formed into a patty and packed into animal skins to sustain a traveler. Pemmican was filled with protein, and the ever-essential vitamin C. Colonists who survived scurvy did so because of the blushing cranberries.

The health benefits of the berry became familiar to the settlers, who learned of their medicinal qualities from the Native Americans. They learned to brew diuretic teas from dried leaves that served to purify the urinary tract. Research today has revealed that the juice from the cranberry, as well as the blueberry, has several health benefits: a compound that inhibits growth in tumors, cleanses the bladder reducing the occurrence of infections, and is an excellent promoter of heart health.

The vines were everywhere in the sandy bogs around the Plymouth Bay Colony. Their bright red color made it easy for the berries to be found by the women and children who handpicked them. Ships were packed with berries to feed the crew on long voyages. Demand for the berry grew and formal cultivation began in 1816 in Dennis, Massachusetts under the watchful eye of Captain Henry Hall. Methods for dry and water harvesting were soon adapted and the cranberry business was born.

Since then, the cranberry has found itself as a staple in the American larder. Whole and jellied cranberry sauce, once invited to the dinner table only at holidays, is spread on bulky deli sandwiches for lunch. Whole berries are chopped into salsas and stewed into chutney, or sweetened and dried to be eaten like raisins. Also, they are baked into muffins or dipped in chocolate for an outrageous candy. Cranberry juice has also stepped into a bold new reality; blends with familiar and exotic fruit have launched it out of its one-dimensional past. As a nation we consume nearly 400 million pounds of cranberries per year.

Grower and entrepreneur John Decas says the Cape Cod cranberry is the best in the country and Massachusetts is among the largest cranberry producers in the world. States like Oregon and countries like Canada are moving fast to catch the wave of popularity the cranberry is enjoying. Government support is making it easy, especially in other countries, to get this agriculturally sound industry moving.

The profiles in this chapter tell the story of berry growers in southeastern Massachusetts. John Decas of Decas Cranberry discusses the realities faced by the Massachusetts cranberry grower, and Jim Ward of Ward's Berry Farm reveals why he has not put all his berries in one basket.

Decas Cranberry Company

The Decas cranberry business began in the mid-1930s under the direction of three Greek immigrant brothers. John Decas, straightforward and at ease, with a countenance that defies any estimation of age, was born into his family business. He attended the University of Massachusetts School of Agriculture when the cranberry industry was unexciting, mostly plodding along. But John loved the farming life and this kept him on his course. Over the years, he has watched and abetted the tremendous growth of the Decas ventures and notes that changing and growing with the industry has determined their success.

The companies own 500 acres; most are in production, about 50 are in rehabilitation. Some 150 Massachusetts growers work under contract with Decas Cranberry Sales, as well as ten in Maine and two in Oregon. This committed owner feels a strong obligation to the growers to receive their fruit, so he must do his best for them. He pitches in at harvest time and works with them to keep up with law and regulation changes, maintaining an open-door policy. Spending the afternoon with John Decas in the excitement and hustle of harvest, I understood that his consuming dedication is about more than keeping up the integrity of the independent farmer. It's about upholding the reputation of the Cape Cod cranberry as superior to any other.

What makes our corner of New England yield a superior berry? The Wareham area boasts ideal conditions for the vines: acidic soil with low nutrients and cool temperatures, even into summer months. John Decas and his growers handle two main berry varieties that are best-suited to the area: early blacks and late howes. Our long, cool growing season and cold, but not extreme, winters contribute to the plant's health all year. The vines blossom in mid June and by late July the berries appear. Ripening continues into autumn. After harvest the bogs are partially flooded so the vines freeze, preventing dry roots, winter kill or wind burn. As the ice melts in spring, the vine awakens to begin its cycle again. John notes that the New England berries are often higher in flavor and acid than the west coast berries (which gain color and sugar more quickly, resulting in low acid content). The acid is what gives the berry its complexity and depth of flavor.

If this region is so marvelously suited for cranberry growing, isn't it the ideal place to be a cranberry grower? After all, most bogs are small family-owned and -operated farms and doing well: Massachusetts is a world leader in cranberry production and generates about 5,000–6,000 jobs. As we drive through the bogs, John Decas explains why his answer is a fast and even "No."

Dean Decas, John's son, working with scoop at Stuart Bog

Joseph D. Thomas

Urban encroachment is the number one problem squeezing the cranberry farmer. Southeastern Massachusetts and Cape Cod have been on the fast-track of urban and suburban development over the last two decades. For every acre of wetland bog, a farmer prefers to manage an additional five acres of woodlands, reservoirs and brush that will act naturally to protect the balance wetlands require. The unpolluted water needed to harvest and protect the crops can be threatened by "nonpoint source pollution" that comes from seeping septic systems and runoff from roadways and landfills. The cost per acre to maintain those buffering lands becomes more difficult as "highest and best" value (determined by its desirability for development) increases, forcing farmers to release lands for sale, leaving them vulnerable to housing developments.

John K. Robson

Corralling berries in South Carver

As neighborhoods and businesses get closer to the bogs, they put pressure on farmers to ban useful pesticides. In response, some manufacturers will not invest the time and money to go through political hoops to renew their products in compliance with state regulations. The cranberry is a low-acre commodity; Massachusetts is just shy of 14,000 planted acres. The widely used integrated pest management practices employed by growers mean pesticide usage is at a minimum. Bugs and rot are still a reality, with or without the pesticides and fungicides. More prolific and disease-resistant berry varieties are in development but the cost of replants, at $20–$30,000 per acre, can be prohibitive.

Dry harvesting with picking machines at Stuart Bog in Rochester

John K. Robson

John stops to examine an area being water harvested, a perfect opportunity to discuss the water situation when a new neighborhood moves in. His son and co-workers have flooded a bog from a holding pond. The beautiful crimson berries have floated to the surface and the boom is in the water. However, on the far side of the bog I notice the water is below the plant tops. John Decas explains: "The water level needs to reach just to the top of the vine to harvest. This is an old field and very uneven, six inches deep on one end, running to two feet on the other. Full flooding requires more water on hand." The long-term solution is a bog rebuild; for example, a large 20-acre field could be divided into four five-acre plots graded six inches lower in each plot, allowing for systematic flooding one plot at a time. The immediate solution requires waiting on the harvest from another bog so water can be pumped through the canal into the uneven bog.

Despite the obstacles, John Decas plans well ahead and sees an exciting future. The market for cranberry products no longer rotates around the holiday season exclusively. Demand for dried berries for snacks, cereals and baking rises continually and the juice market is at full throttle. The new medical research surrounding the health benefits packed by this little red berry may be at the heart of it.

The Decas companies will continue to offer total vertical integration, handling their berries from growth through processing to delivery, expanding to meet the increase in demand. Their dry-harvested berries are packaged as a fresh retail product for the holidays, while the water-harvested fruit is pressed into juices, cooked into jellies, or processed into sweetened dried fruit. Each gets a share of the annual harvest. New value-added products are in research and development as the company seeks to use as much of its own fruit as possible. John Decas smiles as he talks about the accomplishments that have gotten him this far, and about where his tomorrows might take him.

Corralled berries are raked into a conveyor and onto a truck during wet harvest, South Carver.

John K. Robson

Ward's Berry Farm

Ward's Berry Farm is in its second and third generations. The birth parents of this business in Sharon, Massachusetts are William Arthur and Ann Ward. William, a devoted home gardener, bought the 30-acre property after retiring from a fruitful career as a scientist, electrical engineer and inventor. He pulled up the scrub cedar that covered the sandy, acidic soil and, by 1981, he had planted 3,000 blueberry bushes and, a year later, 3,000 more. The first berries were harvested in 1983. He also grew strawberries and corn, transacting the first sales off the back of the family pickup. The next year he constructed a farmstand on the foundation of a house whose days had passed.

The elder Mr. Ward held fast to what was most important to him—selling quality, which meant selling produce only on the day it was picked. This practice is maintained by William Ward's children and grandchildren who have continued to manage the farm since his death in 1985. Jim, one of the seven Ward children, oversees most of the farm's daily activities and is constantly reminded of his father's commitment to quality. One of his favorite childhood memories includes a ritual his parents performed nightly, when the garden corn was full in the ear. His mother would have the pot of water boiling—waiting while his father was picking and shucking. The reward for their diligence was the richest, sweetest, most flavorful corn—butter not needed.

The desire to make things grow seems to be in the genes of each family member, and they bring their individual talents to the task at hand. Sisters Barbara, Pat, Joyce, and Julie all have full and busy lives, but they make time to pitch in, designing and assembling bulk mailings, baking, keeping the family's recipes safe in the computer. The morning of my visit, Barbara's son Andrew arrived early for his first day on the job filling orders. He was set to the task of bagging corn and bunching sunflowers immediately; deliveries would go out around 8AM.

Ward Berry Farm farmstand in Sharon

Joseph D. Thomas

Brother Bill recently returned to the area with his family, committing himself to weekends, but he is around almost daily before and after work. His children Emily and Billy are employed by the Berry Farm. Jim and Bob are the official business partners, each lending his strengths to the operation. Bob runs the business end of things: assessing numbers, evaluating markets and pursuing new directions and outlets. Jim, who traded in his engineering studies for a degree in plant and soil science from the University of Massachusetts, clicked easily into position as the farm's manager; overseer of employees, of planting and harvesting, of exploring new crops and improving the old.

Fresh berries at the Ward farmstand

Growth and diversity have marked the years since the farm began. William Ward saw the future in blueberries, and the berry patch now boasts 7,000 bushes. He did not see turning acreage over to raising corn, as the space required is sizable. The family leases an additional 125 acres to accommodate several plantings of half a dozen varieties of corn, pumpkins, squash, tomatoes and zucchini to sell at the farmstand. Jim and Bob have also increased their connection to the community. A play area, which includes a sandbox and tractors, is open to the public on and off-season. Hayrides begin in October with the plants as the featured attractions. The demand is greater than they expected with tours running all day almost every day.

When asked about getting his berries into the baskets of the public, Jim Ward echoed the sentiments of other farmers. "The current state of the market limits wholesale and forces

Shopping at Ward Berry Farm farmstand

Joseph D. Thomas

the need for retail or direct sales to stores and restaurants." His tone and countenance are friendly, even, and his smile is easy as he discusses the challenges he faces daily. He is happy to explain the current strategies his family has made to get out there.

Berry Farm produce is taken to the Chelsea and Providence markets weekly and can be purchased on the farm. He enjoys watching shoppers and notes a greater willingness on their part to try a new variety of old favorites. They seem willing to experiment with fresh herbs, funky peppers and up to seven types of eggplant. The inclination of the consumer to choose "big and blemish free" over real flavor and freshness as quality standards is still an obstacle. But educating the public is a driving force for Jim. This is where the cooperative effort serves him well. Organized marketing programs keep the farmer more in touch with the buyers. Brand identification associated with quality standards will create demand, and the strength of a cooperative means a stronger voice in the price. He is very excited about Coastal Growers Association's potted herb program and will become more involved in it in the future, making use of his greenhouse space when not in use as the nursery for the year's crops.

I had the pleasure of meeting three generations of Wards involved with the farm. A highlight for me as a chef was spending time in their commercial kitchen talking with the farm's head baker, Ann Ward. While we chatted about recipes and family traditions, Mrs. Ward moved about the kitchen almost effortlessly, wearing the same sincere smile as her son, expertly rolling butter and flour through her fingertips, stopping only to open the convection oven and rotate a batch of enormous blueberry muffins and slide in a strawberry crisp. She handed me a warm muffin. Seeing my eyes widen as I thanked her, she told me why these buttery breakfast treats were so large. "People turn off the highway for my muffins. They should be worth the stop. A real breakfast." This Italian-born woman will never sell you yesterday's goods. For her, fresh baking is another way to care for their customers. When I asked her about the changes she has seen in their growing family farm, she responded, "Dad would be proud."

In Search of Cranberry Pie

If your acquaintance with cranberry pie has been made in a restaurant or hotel dining room, I do not blame you for not cultivating a taste for it…it is a sad affair…But a real cranberry pie—a homemade, home-baked cranberry pie, prepared by a Cape Cod kitchen artist of the old school is different, gloriously different. — Joseph C. Lincoln, *Cape Cod Yesterdays*

Unfortunately, I am ignorant of the realities of a true cranberry pie; I have never tasted one. I have used cranberries baked in a crust with apples, blueberries or pecans but never made a cranberry-only pie. I am now in search of one, preferably from one of those old-school Cape Cod kitchen artists.

The author of *Cape Cod Yesterdays* hinted at what the proper formula should include. "I have a dim memory that in our house…a cranberry pie was sweetened with brown sugar, the moist lumpy kind. In Grandmother's youth, it was, of course, sweetened with molasses." The story also states that a true cranberry pie is made with whole, fresh berries that go into the crust uncooked.

If any reader has such a recipe and would like to share it, I am intrigued and would like to make and taste it. To contact me, please write c/o the publisher. Thank you.

Handling Fresh Berries

Old cranberry barrel label from Betty's Neck in Rochester

Wash all varieties of fresh berries just before using in a colander under cool running water. A wet berry will become mushy in the refrigerator. If you do not plan to cook fresh cranberries right away, they will freeze beautifully and keep frozen for several months.

Cranberry Sauce

1 lb. cranberries
⅓ cup sugar
¾ cup fresh apple juice

There is nothing like warm cranberry sauce to change the atmosphere around a simple roasted chicken and rice dinner. Chilled and spread on a deli sandwich or stirred into warm oatmeal are other options for this versatile condiment.

Combine the ingredients in a stainless sauce pot and simmer over a medium-low flame for about 8 minutes until the cranberries have burst. Serve warm or cool. Can be stored in the refrigerator for several weeks.

MAKES ABOUT 2 CUPS.

Gathering dry-harvested berries, Stuart Bog, Rochester

John K. Robson

Sautéed Chicken with Cranberries and Apple Cider Reduction

Served with roasted potatoes or buttered rice with freshly steamed green beans will make a full plate.

Dust the chicken with flour, one at a time, shaking off any excess. Heat the oil in a large sauté pan over medium-high heat, then sauté the chicken until golden brown on both sides and thoroughly cooked, 3–5 minutes each side. Transfer the chicken to a serving platter and hold warm. Pour off any remaining oil. Put the pan back on the heat and toss in the shallots and cranberries. Cook for 2 minutes. Add stock and wine, bring to a low boil and reduce volume by half. Stir in sugar and cider and reduce by half. Stir in butter and season to taste with salt. Pour over chicken breasts.

MAKES 4 SERVINGS.

Stephen Worden, Worden's 7 Water Street Restaurant, Dartmouth, MA

4 6-oz. boneless chicken breasts
¼ cup flour
¼ cup oil
1 tbsp. shallots, peeled and chopped
½ cup cranberries, chopped
½ cup chicken stock
¼ cup white wine
1 tbsp. sugar
¼ cup apple cider
2 tbsp. unsalted butter
Salt

Cranberry Chutney

Take orange sections out of the skin and cut in small chunks. Combine all ingredients in 3-quart pan and simmer until cranberries pop and are cooked. They will look glossy when ready. Serve warm or chilled. Will keep several weeks in the refrigerator.

MAKES 4 CUPS.

Lois H. Simon, Westport, MA,

3 small oranges
2 cups sugar
½ cup raisins
¼ cup chopped walnuts
½ tsp. ginger
4 cups cranberries
1 cup chopped unpeeled apple
½ cup orange juice
1 tbsp. white cider vinegar
½ tsp. cinnamon

Water harvest in South Carver

John K. Robson

Rich and Chewy Cranberry White Chocolate Cookies

2/3 cup unsalted butter, melted and cooled until slightly warmed
1½ cups light brown sugar
2 tbsp. honey
1 large egg
2 tsp. vanilla
2 cups all-purpose flour
½ cup old-fashioned oats
½ tsp. baking soda
½ tsp. salt
½ tsp. cinnamon
¾ cup white chocolate chips
1 cup sweetened dried cranberries
½ cup chopped toasted hazelnuts or pecans

Preheat oven to 350°. By hand or mixer, blend together butter, brown sugar and honey. Add egg and vanilla and mix well. In a large bowl, stir together flour, oats, soda, salt and cinnamon; add to butter mixture and mix just until combined. Stir in remaining ingredients.

Place 1½" pieces of dough 2" apart on ungreased baking sheet and bake in center of oven until edges are lightly browned and centers are still soft, about 12–15 minutes. Do not overbake. Cool completely.

MAKES 2½ DOZEN COOKIES.

Paradise Meadow Cranberries, Wareham, MA

Water harvest, South Carver

John K. Robson

Cranberry Walnut Pie

Preheat oven to 375°. In a saucepan, bring the cider to a boil over high heat; reduce heat to medium, add sugar and stir; add cranberries and cook for 10 minutes. Pour in melted butter and stir well; allow mixture to cool. In a large bowl, beat the eggs until frothy, pour in cooled cider, cranberry mixture and lemon juice; stir again and add walnuts. Pour entire mixture into pie shell. Bake for 30 minutes or until center of pie is firm. Serve warm or at room temperature.

MAKES ONE 9" PIE.

Paradise Meadow Cranberries, Wareham, MA

1 butter-flavored ready crust
1½ cups sweet apple cider
1 cup light brown sugar
1 cup fresh or frozen cranberries, chopped
4 tbsp. butter, melted
4 eggs, beaten
2 tsp. lemon juice
½ cup walnuts, finely chopped

Cranberry Granola

Preheat oven to 375°. On a cookie sheet, spread the oats and germ out in a thin layer. Toast until slightly golden, about 7-10 minutes. In a large bowl, mix the flakes, cranberries, nuts and coconut together, crunching the flakes a few times in your hands. Warm the juice and stir in the honey to dissolve. Lower the oven to 325°. Stir the oat mixture into the flake mixture. Pour the juice and honey over the top and fold it in. Line the cookie sheet with parchment or foil and lightly spray with canola oil spray. Spread the granola out on the pan in an even layer. Bake for 15-18 minutes, stirring once. Cool completely and store in an airtight container. Serve as is, with milk, or stirred into yogurt for a quick energy snack.

MAKES 6 CUPS

2 cups rolled oats
1 cup raw wheat germ
1 cup cereal flakes, preferably bran or corn
1 cup sweetened dried cranberries
½ cup chopped walnuts or pecans
½ cup sweetened flaked coconut
⅓ cup orange or pineapple juice
3 tbsp. honey

Corralling berries in South Carver

John K. Robson

Cranberry Nut Bread

1½ tsp. baking powder
2 cups flour
½ tsp. soda
½ tsp. salt
1 cup sugar
1 cup cranberries, cut into halves
½ cup chopped nutmeats
1 well-beaten egg
Juice of 1 orange, plus warm
    water to make 1 cup
3 tbsp. melted shortening

Preheat oven to 350°. Sift all dry ingredients together. Add cranberries and nutmeats. Then add egg mixed with diluted orange juice and shortening, stir until just combined. Bake in greased and floured loaf pan for 1 hour.

MAKES 1 LOAF PAN.

Paradise Meadow Cranberries, Wareham, MA

Cranberry-Orange Relish

3 cups cranberries
1 orange
1½ cups sugar

Put cranberries through meat grinder. Pare orange and remove seeds and white membrane. Put rind and pulp through grinder, then mix with sugar and berries. Let stand a few hours before serving. In the absence of a meat grinder, pulse in a food processor until the cranberries are in small pieces.

MAKES 2 PINTS.

Paradise Meadow Cranberries, Wareham, MA

Preparing to lift crates of berries "ashore"

John K. Robson

Strawberry-Orange Shortcake

Put the strawberries and oranges in a bowl, sprinkle with sugar and vanilla, toss and hold in the refrigerator.

Stir the lemon juice into the cream and hold at room temperature.

Sift together the flour, cinnamon, baking powder and salt in a large mixing bowl and toss in the cubed butter to coat. Combine using your fingers, rolling the flour and butter over your fingertips with your thumbs until the mixture resembles a coarse meal. Pour in half of the cream mixture and work in gently with your hands. Add more cream as needed until the dough forms a ball. Do not overwork or allow it to get tacky. Wrap the dough and let it rest at room temperature for 15 minutes.

Preheat the oven to 425°. Roll out the shortcake dough on a lightly floured surface and cut with a 2–3" round cutter. Scraps can be re-rolled once, or baked as they are, for snacking. Sprinkle the top of each shortcake biscuit with sugar. Place sugar side up on a sprayed cookie sheet 1" apart and bake for 12–15 minutes until puffed and golden. Cool on a rack and split in half. Beat the cream in a chilled bowl until it begins to thicken, stream in the sugar while mixing and continue to beat until the cream holds soft peaks.

To assemble: Spoon a generous serving of fruit and juices over the bottom half of a biscuit set in the center of a dessert dish. Dollop the cream over the fruit and set the biscuit top on the cream and press down gently, allowing the cream and fruit to squish out the sides.

MAKES 6 SERVINGS.

1½ cups halved strawberries
2 oranges, ends cut, knife-peeled, sliced in pinwheels, then cut in half
1 tsp. granulated sugar
¼ tsp. vanilla
½ cup heavy cream
2 tbsp. lemon juice
1¾ cups unbleached flour
1 tsp. cinnamon
1 tbsp. baking powder
Pinch salt
4 oz. butter, cut in ½" cubes
1 cup whipping cream
¼ cup confectioners' sugar

John K. Robson

Grading the truckload

Scooper dumps his berries in the crate, Stuart Bog, Rochester.

John K. Robson

Really Lemon Mousse

2 eggs
1½ cups sugar
Pinch salt
1½ tbsp. cornstarch
1 cup fresh lemon juice
1 cup whipping cream
1½ tsp. vanilla
1½ tbsp. honey

This mousse has intense flavor. Spoon it over raspberries or blackberries and serve with your favorite butter cookie.

Whisk the eggs with the sugar, cornstarch and salt, then whisk in lemon juice. Pour into a stainless or enamel sauce pot. Cook over medium-low heat stirring continuously with a wooden spoon until thickened. The mixture should coat the back of a wooden spoon. Remove from the heat and pour into a bowl to cool, cover and chill. When cooled completely, beat the cream until foamy with a whisk or electric mixer. Stream in the vanilla and honey while beating, then continue until the cream holds a soft peak. Fold into the lemon mixture in two additions. Store chilled in the refrigerator up to 2 days.

MAKES 2½ CUPS.

Mrs. Downing's Blueberry Bread

2 eggs
1 cup sugar
1 cup milk
¼ cup melted butter
3 cups flour
1 tsp. salt
4 tsp. baking powder
1 cup blueberries, tossed in 1 tsp. flour

A special recipe given to Mrs. Ward by her very dear friend.

Preheat oven to 350°. Beat eggs with sugar, milk and butter. Combine dry ingredients and pour in egg mixture, stirring gently. Stir in blueberries. Pour into 2 greased loaf pans (or small muffin tins). Sprinkle the tops with sugar. Bake 40–50 minutes for loaves, 20–25 minutes for muffins.

MAKES 2 LOAVES.

Ward's Berry Farm, Sharon, MA

Jim Ward and his trusty old tractor, Ward's Berry Farm

Joseph D. Thomas

Blueberry Muffins

The early morning I drove out to Ward's, I neglected to eat breakfast. I thankfully accepted one of these tender muffins straight from the oven...delicious!

Preheat oven to 350°. If you forgot to soften the butter, melt it, but don't allow it to brown. Put butter and sugar in the mixing bowl and beat at low speed for several seconds, until mixed. Add eggs one at a time and beat after each addition until incorporated. Add vanilla and mix. Add salt, baking powder, and half of the flour and beat on low speed until incorporated. Now add half of the milk and mix until incorporated. Add remaining flour and milk, mixing in after each addition. Do not overmix. Once the mixture is homogeneous, you are done. Overbeating makes the muffin tough. Remove bowl from mixer.

Pick over the blueberries, wash them if necessary, sprinkle a little extra flour on them, and toss to coat them in flour. Add the blueberries to the batter and mix in gently by hand.

Spray non-stick spray into muffin tins. Scoop batter into tins. Sprinkle a little sugar on top of each muffin.

Bake for about 20 minutes. To test for doneness, stick a toothpick in the center of a muffin. If the toothpick comes out clean (with no batter stuck to it), the muffins are done. If the toothpick went through a blueberry, then it's not a fair test—try again.

MAKES 6 JUMBO OR 12 LARGE MUFFINS.

Ann Ward, Ward's Berry Farm, Sharon, MA

1 stick butter, softened
1 cup sugar
2 large eggs
1 tsp. vanilla (optional)
2 cups flour
2 tsp. baking powder
½ tsp. salt
½ cup milk
1 cup blueberries
A little extra sugar and flour

Joseph D. Thomas

Fresh berries at Ward's farmstand

Dan Minihan gathering blueberries at Ward's farm

Joseph D. Thomas

Blueberry Buckle

3 cups blueberries, stemmed
  and washed
2 tbsp. sugar
1 stick or 4 oz. butter, softened
¾ cup sugar
1 egg beaten
½ tsp. pure vanilla extract
1½ cups all-purpose flour
2 tsp. baking powder
½ tsp. salt
½ cup milk

Joseph D. Thomas

This recipe can also be made with apples, pears, peaches, or raspberries but tastes best with wild blueberries. The aroma of this baking sends me back to Nantucket and childhood summers. The day after my brothers, sisters and I picked the berries, we would wake to the smell of coffee percolating and this buttery blueberry pastry.

Preheat oven to 350°. Put 2 tablespoons of the butter into the 9" dish and place in oven (a well-seasoned cast iron skillet is preferred). Combine the berries with 2 tablespoons sugar. In a mixer, beat the remaining butter and sugar on medium-high speed until light in color. Beat in the egg and vanilla until thoroughly incorporated. Sift together the flour, baking powder and salt. Turn the mixer to low speed and add the dry ingredients alternately with the milk in two parts, until just combined. Stir the sugared berries into the preheated pan and pour the batter over the top. Place immediately in oven and bake for 20–25 minutes until the edges are golden brown and it is set in the center. Remove from oven and set to cool for 10 minutes. It is best served immediately, as is for breakfast, or with a dollop of sweetened whipped cream as a scrumptious dessert.

MAKES ONE 9" DEEP DISH PIE.

Betse V. Downey, Dartmouth, MA

Young harvesters pick their own berries at Ward's Berry Farm

John K. Robson

Chocolate Berry Shortcake

Shortcake is a favorite in this region. This is the second of two very different recipes (see page 99), which makes use of our wonderful local berries. Both biscuits can be made well in advance and stored frozen, cut and uncooked.

Combine the milk and lemon juice and set aside at room temperature. In a separate bowl, sift the dry ingredients together 2 times. Toss the butter into the dry mixture to coat the cubes, then roll the butter between your fingers until the mixture resembles coarse meal. Add half the milk and lemon and work in quickly and gently with a wooden spoon. Add more milk and lemon as needed until the dough holds together and is softened. Wrap and chill the dough for 20 minutes.

Preheat oven to 425°. Roll out the dough on a lightly floured surface to ½" thickness. Sprinkle the top with sugar and cut. Set 1" apart on a cookie sheet lined with parchment paper and bake for 10 minutes, or until golden, turning pan around after 5 minutes. Cool completely on a rack. Split in half and fill with whipped cream or ice cream and washed berries. Extra biscuits can be frozen up to a week.

MAKES 1 DOZEN 2" BISCUITS.

½ cup nonfat milk
1 tbsp. lemon juice
1½ cups all-purpose flour
½ cup cocoa powder
¼ tsp. salt
¼ cup sugar
1 tbsp. plus 1 tsp. baking powder
4 oz. sweet butter, cut into small cubes
Granulated sugar
Fresh raspberries, blueberries, strawberries—⅓ cup per serving

Betse Downey

Red raspberries

Simple Blueberry Pie

Judy says this is the easiest and most enjoyable pie she's ever made.

Mix together sugar, cornstarch, salt and water. Line baked shell with 2 cups dry blueberries. In sauce pan cook remaining blueberries with all other ingredients except butter. Cook until thick. Remove from heat and add butter, cool. Pour over berries in shell. Cool slightly.

MAKES ONE 9" OR 10" PIE.

Judy Rebello, Fisher Farm, Dartmouth, MA

1 cup sugar
1 tbsp. cornstarch
¼ tsp. salt
¼ cup water
1 baked pie shell, 9" or 10"
4 cups fresh blueberries
1 tbsp. butter

CHAPTER SIX

Grapes for Wine

*It was shown them (the natives) in pressing the grape into a glass that
we did make the wine of which we did drink. We would have made
them drink of the wine, but having taken it into their mouths, they
spitted it out...the best thing God hath given to man next to bread.*
– Marc Lescarbot, Champlain Expedition along Massachusetts in 1606.

*We could in the United States make as great a variety of wines
as are made in Europe...* — Thomas Jefferson

Wild grapes were among this coast's special gems. Leafy vines clung
to trees in woods, or bent over the aging trunks that gripped into the sands by
water's edge. The berries were round and plump and the juice was sweet.
Native Americans loved grapes for their sweetness, eating them fresh in early
fall and drying them for winter use. The practice of squeezing grapes to allow
their own wild yeasts to convert their sugars to alcohol arrived with the settlers.

Sakonnet Vineyards, Little Compton

John K. Robson

"For he that loveth wine, wanteth no woes," wrote Anne Bradstreet, Puritan poet and first American woman writer, in *Of the Four Ages of Man.* Fermentation was a common thing to the European. The juice from apples, pears, and grapes was pressed to make "cyder," perry and wine. The Christian settler drank them with meals, sipped them warm to take the chill off, or used them as medicines. Excess was unacceptable.

John K. Robson

> *Drink in itself is a good creature of God and to be received with thankfulness, but the abuse of drink is from Satan. The wine is from God but the drunkard is from the devil.* — Increase Mather, American Minister, 1639-1723.

Westport Rivers Vineyard

Wines from the New World grape (concord was the most common) were being produced in the Massachusetts Bay Colony in the 1630s. However, they were not very good. This unfamiliar grape was better for jellies or eaten right off the vine. The classic European vines, *vitis vinifera,* were the world's standard with such names as pinot noir, riesling and chardonnay.

Planting the old world *vitis vinifera* roots in the new soil failed miserably. Our east coast earth was home to a hungry, hearty little grub called *phylloxera vastatrix* that dined voraciously on the roots of vinifera vines. In fact, many of the vineyards of France had been nearly devastated by 1864 as native American grapes were brought overseas for similar adaptability experiments. Grafting the vinifera grapes onto the grub-resistant American rootstocks saved the French vineyards and signaled the beginning of successful plantings and a new American venture.

The next blow to budding vineyards and wineries came in 1919—Prohibition. Vineyards were plowed under and replaced by other crops, or wineries produced sacramental wines or juice concentrates and thus survived. An entire generation went without wine until the Repeal in 1933. Demand was low for fine wines, so the bulk wine industry began.

No one in New England made any concerted effort to grow grapes for winemaking until the mid 1960s, and it was not until 1974 that anyone regionally stepped up to the plate. Jim and Lolly Mitchell opened Sakonnet Vineyards in Little Compton, Rhode Island, by planting hybrid vines to make their own wines.

The first interview in this chapter is with Joetta Kirk, Sakonnet's viticulturist. Her story of the winery's progression in the vineyard and through the transfer of ownership is our own regional viticultural history in the making.

Several other farms turned their soils over to grape growing on the heels of the Mitchells, but none were set up to make wine. But early in the 1980s, Bob and Carol Russell sold their Dighton home and his company to begin a business they could share together: a vineyard and winery. They found this coastal region between Marion and Little Compton to be the sunniest and most temperate in New England. They purchased the 110-acre Smith-Long Acre farm in Westport, Massachusetts, for their home and business (the property had been a farm since its original purchase) and began to work toward their dream. Westport Rivers Vineyard and Winery was born.

Their son, Rob Russell, is the second featured grower in the chapter. He joined his family business to manage their vineyards and has not looked back. The farm has recently grown to 200 acres and the business is also branching out into a farm brewery, but that's another story.

Both vineyards are now making top-quality wines that are turning the heads of consumers and critics alike. The European varietals of chardonnay, pinot noir, riesling and others adapted beautifully to the south-eastern New England climate—bud break in mid May and first frost between mid October into November. This long growing season

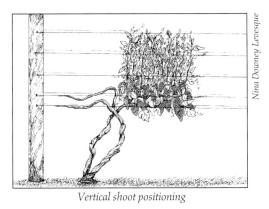

Vertical shoot positioning

means that the grapes can ripen (develop sugar) and mature (reach proper color and skin development, and proper fruit-in-the-mouth characteristics) at the same rate.

As a matter of fact, certain aspects of our climate mirror those of the Mosel in Germany, which produces lush and spicy riesling, and the chablis in France, which is noted for clean, crisp fruity chardonnays, and Champagne, France! Surprised? This lovely, seaside area is a great place to grow grapes for world-class sparkling wines. Westport Rivers celebrated their fifth release of *Methode Champenoise* (or classically produced sparkling wines made in the traditional French manner) in 1998 and are looking forward to pressing nearly half of their annual harvests into beautiful bubblies. They currently grow and produce estate blanc de blancs, brut, a sparkling riesling and a blanc de noirs. The Westport sparkling wines are acknowledged as some of the finest in the United States. Sakonnet Vineyards will also be releasing traditional-method sparkling wines in the coming years.

Both growers attribute the success of vine growth to the climate, but also to their "canopy" management of Vertical Shoot Positioning (VSP). From bottom to top (the simplified version): the vine may consist of one or two trunks, with two canes tied to the left and right of the vine onto two tie wires or fruiting wires. This section is where all the fruit grows in the vine. For every foot of cane on the trellis, there should be an average of five to six buds. From these buds, shoots emerge that bear the fruit and foliage of the vines. The shoots are then trained upwards through a series of three movable catch wires. As the shoot grows over one wire, the next is moved upwards to keep the leaves from shading the grapes. After the vines have reached the third wire, they are "hedged," clipped off the top and sides so air moves freely through the vines to reduce fungal problems and the sun can shine on the fruit. If you've ever visited the warmer wine regions in California, you'll notice that the "canopy" is allowed to grow over the grapes, to a certain degree, to prevent the hot, dry sun from ripening the fruit (make sugar) before maturity. VSP requires that the vines be pruned in the winter months when the vinegrower will choose which will be the canes for the following year. A vineyard is unique in farming as it is not handled by the acre or by crop type, but each vine is known intimately.

Sakonnet Vineyards and Westport Rivers Vineyard and Winery are both looking far into a very promising future. They are enjoying the fruits of their labor, successful both in farming and in making wine. Both wineries are open for tours and run their own retail outlets. More growers are planting and perhaps other wineries will be established. In the meantime, Joetta Kirk and Rob Russell will keep moving ahead, testing the capacity of this farm coast's capabilities to grow the greatest grapes.

Sakonnet Vineyards

When does a career begin? For Joetta Kirk, the life of a viticulturist began in Sakonnet's vineyards in her mid-thirties, or did it? I met Joetta, bright, welcoming and full of energy, one unseasonably warm December day to find out. She passed on her pruning shears and the task of clipping buds for grafting to her assistant and led me to her office with a beautiful view of the vineyards, where we could talk. Among the stacks of vineyard records, reference materials and tractor manuals we discussed how this country girl became a grape-farmer.

Joetta's grandparents on her mother's side were farmers. She spent her early childhood years in a country community like Dartmouth, playing outdoors and helping in the garden. She remembers the family car trips through upstate New York, pressing her face against the window in fascination as they passed tidy rows of grape vines. Hers are happy memories in western Pennsylvania of open space, things green, warm summers and cold winters. "From eleven on, I grew up in Coastal New Hampshire, leaving the country life behind. Bike riding, going to the beach and playing in the woods were normal things to do."

As a young woman, it never occurred to Joetta that farming was something she even liked. All she had enjoyed about "dirty work" was kid stuff. During her 20s, she took jobs in hairdressing, retail, secretarial work and freelance advertising while moving through areas like Buffalo, Booth Bay, Brattleboro and Boston. Eventually she landed on a gentleman's farm in Canton, Massachusetts, where Joetta exchanged part-time work for housing. The supposed not-so-ladylike life of farming, she discovered, was right for her, and her part-time job became full-time.

Early summer vines at Sakonnet Vineyards

John K. Robson

A drive down West Main Road in Little Compton in 1983 brought Ms. Kirk into the entrance of the eight-year-old Sakonnet Vineyards and, purely by chance, an introduction to owners Jim and Lolly Mitchell. After three meetings Joetta was asked to come to work. Although she knew nothing about viticulture she could drive the tractor and fix it too. After a year and a half, she exhibited such diligence and commitment to the job that she was promoted to vineyard manager. She learned her techniques from Jim Mitchell. The vineyard came to a crucial point several years later and the Mitchells put the vineyard and winery up for sale.

Joseph D. Thomas

Joetta Kirk

In 1987, a new era began for Sakonnet Vineyards under the ownership of Earl and Susan Samson. Joetta was sent to New Zealand to attend a cool-climate viticultural seminar. "For the first time I was surrounded by colleagues from all over the world and I was introduced to Vertical Shoot Positioning." She also learned that some of the hybrid varietals that she tended could be replaced with vinifera plants, which would yield better-quality grapes. She set to the task of changing the trellis system immediately and began the slow process of replants.

The last ten years have seen much change in Sakonnet's vineyards, from improved vine spacing to the planting of new varietals: gewurztraminer, cabernet franc, cabernet sauvignon, and merlot in addition to chardonnay, chancellor and vidal. During this stretch of time, Joetta's knowledge of vine care and her own vineyards has grown. "What makes this site special?" I asked her. Her eyes lit up and an excitement rose in her voice. "Jim Mitchell was brilliant in choosing this plot of land. The vineyard is a dome so air moves through the rows and the soil is well-drained, but holds enough water. There is river and ocean all around us so the air is constantly moving." This keeps cold air and frost from settling on the plants. Fog, however, is a concern. With moisture comes fungus and potential damage to foliage and fruit. What would make the vineyard ideal? Joetta would change the direction of the east/west running rows to north/south and plant varietals block by block instead of row by row.

The daily managing of the vines is exciting to this viticulturist. Joetta enjoys her discussions with Westport Rivers' Rob Russell and learns a lot from him. "Our (vine management) styles complement each other." The risks Rob takes and the careful planning Ms. Kirk employs often combine to solve a mutual problem our cool, often damp, climate presents. "Rob and I discuss challenges for hours. We have learned to address them together. Compared to drier areas (these vineyards) require continuous handling." Her focus is not quantity only; uniqueness and quality from each variety are what she's after.

Instinctively, Joetta does not put "all her eggs in one basket." Instead, she thoroughly tests her theories. Her experimentation with red grapes has

Fermentation tanks at Sakonnet

Joseph D. Thomas

yielded some interesting results, with cabernet franc responding the best. "I will watch and give each varietal time." As the vineyard evolves, the business is being redefined; what gets a good foothold in the vineyard will eventually end up in the bottle. She is constantly encouraged by her employers, who respect her vision.

John K. Robson

Standing in the middle of row upon row of thriving vines, it's easy for me to see Joetta's influence on the vineyard, but how has this farming life changed her? She has learned to enjoy all aspects of her job, she says. She loves the quietness and separation from the mainstream, being outdoors and connecting so closely with her work. Giving interviews and public speaking were new to her, but she is developing and growing. "It is a challenge to convey information so people can receive it and be excited by it."

Sakonnet Vineyards

What sort of advice would she give someone in our region interested in viticulture as a career? Joetta would stress that this is not a part-time hobby or partial commitment but full-time mental and physical labor. Therefore, one must have a passion for the work in order to rejuvenate a frequently depleted spirit. She agrees that this area is suited for grape growing but one should evaluate a site thoroughly before making a decision to grow grapes. A good site should not require a dramatic rebuild to accommodate a vineyard.

Joetta hopes that the area will become stronger in viticulture and agriculture as a whole. The life may be difficult but the rewards are great, reaching beyond the individual into the community. For her there is no half way, only total involvement. What she reaps from her seeds of diligence is an abundance of joy and satisfaction.

Early spring vines at Sakonnet Vineyards

Joseph D. Thomas

Westport Rivers Vineyard and Winery

I have seen vineyards in many places: covering the floor of the Napa Valley, rolling along the slow hills of Virginia, North Carolina and Pennsylvania, standing against the winds on Long Island, even gripping the steep cliffs on the Amalfi Coast. Still, no vineyard has ever moved me like the sight of Westport's vineyards with their beauty and serenity. My husband, son and I moved here several years ago from the Napa Valley. Though we enjoyed our life in California wine country and would miss being surrounded by vines, Dartmouth was home to us and we decided this region was best for our family. When I read about the Russell family growing vinifera grapes to make traditional sparkling wines right next door in Westport, I couldn't wait to meet them. I quickly made an appointment. The family was there to meet and greet me: owners Bob and Carol Russell and their sons Bill and Rob, vintner and viticulturist, respectively.

This initial introduction led to a whole new chapter in my life. Today, as the executive chef at Westport Rivers, involved in food and wine education, I have been most richly blessed through my experience with the Russell family. Energy, diligence, commitment to excellence and integrity are characteristics they all share. Rob Russell brings these qualities to his job as vineyard manager.

Tall and pony-tailed with a ready smile, Robert James Russell lives and breathes his work. Young Robby Russell grew up in Dighton, Massachusetts with his two younger brothers and younger sister, their property abutting a large vegetable farm. He was intrigued by the tractors and farm equipment as they moved earth, dug rows and harvested crops next

George Phipps, last day of mechanical harvesting in late October at Westport Rivers Vineyard

Joseph D. Thomas

door. The most-employed toy he owned was a red drive-around tractor. As he grew, his interests changed and building things captured his teenage attention. Rob chose Wentworth Institute to pursue his degree in architectural engineering, thinking he would one day design and build custom homes.

While in college, he received an offer from his father to work in the budding family business, a farm and winery in Westport, Massachusetts. Rob weighed his options carefully, decided against the field of construction but also felt he needed some experience if he were to accept his father's offer. He headed for Long Island and took a general worker's job with Fred Frank in the vineyards at Villa Banfi. "It was there I was exposed to all aspects of vineyard work," he said. In 1985, at 21, young Mr. Russell moved to Westport to begin his new career on the former Smith Long Acre farm.

His first task was to fix up an old farmhouse on the dairy farm to make it habitable, then it was transforming former vegetable fields into a vineyard. He began with a post-hole digger to mark the rows for plants. How did it go? "Let's just say that post-hole digger worked in Long Island but was not suited to our rockier soil." His smile is sheepish, if not slightly embarrassed, as he recalls the memory.

A decade plus is behind him now since those first challenging days. What has Rob learned? "I know less than when I started! The more I learn, the more I realize how little I know now." He is referring to the year-round handling of the vines: grafting, planting, protecting, feeding, tying and trellising, trimming, harvesting and pruning. Most recently, the viticulturist has focused on soil health.

His aim is to keep the vines in a low-stress environment, which allows for more prolific and better-quality fruit. (We could learn a lot from a grapevine!) With the vineyard so close to the water, frost or heat-stress is minimized, but mildews love the humid atmosphere. A

Hand harvesting for sparkling wine at Westport Rivers Vineyard

healthy, well-fed vine resists this pressure more successfully. He used fertilization, cover-cropping, and composting but the plants behaved less heartily than desired. Todd Mason, a cool-climate horticulture and viticulture soils expert from Ontario, showed Rob he needed to dig deeper. The pair discovered that the soil was lean on nutrients and too well-drained. There were no energy reserves when the plant needed a boost. A new balance of nutrition, drainage and aeration was prescribed. In one season, Rob has seen a dramatic improvement.

The process of gaining information would be simpler if this were a grape-growing community. Fortunately, he has a solid relationship with Sakonnet's viticulturalist Joetta Kirk and learns much from her methodical style of handling vines. They discuss at length their experiences over weekly phone calls. Their sense of isolation forces them both to look outside for knowledge, experiment extensively and keep exchanging their successes and failures. Rob Russell is grateful they are in this together.

What about the future of Westport Rivers? Rob attributes the strength of the business today, and the bright promise of tomorrow, to the foresight of his father, Bob Russell. Chardonnay, pinot noir and riesling varietals grafted onto Phylloxera-resistant rootstock planted in Westport's vineyards are well-suited to our cool climate and the moderate "meso-climate" specific to the location of this riverside vineyard. The 200-acre farm will reach capacity in 1999, at 77 acres planted with 1100 vines per acre. This will include the original varieties plus pinot blanc, pinot meuniere and pinot gris. Of course, a few acres will be set aside for experimentation.

Does this whole area have the same potential for success? "I see the region as viticulturally sound," says Rob. "There's a lot of promise, but housing and commercial

Rob Russell inspects the late Spring vines.

John K. Robson

development is the biggest hindrance. A lot of potentially good sites are untilled," which requires a big initial investment of time and money. The sight of fallow farmland is a crime to Rob because of its vulnerability. "The decline of a beautiful area feels preventable." He is encouraged by potential buyers with long-term vision who have come to him for advice about farming grapes for wine. Still there is much to be done. Rob shares the view of his contemporaries that local and federal protection of agricultural lands would encourage the growth and profitability of all kinds of farming.

Grapes ready to press for wines

The course Westport Rivers Vineyard and Winery has taken enforces the view that farming can be profitable. The Russells reach the public directly through a retail store that offers tours and tastings. Wine made on the premises gives the business the "value-added" benefit. The crop is not sold elsewhere but handled right in the winery, and quality as well as profit is managed by the business.

Personally, Robert James Russell III has much to look forward to. He and his wife Mardi have a growing family and he relishes the day-to-day excitement of a job that requires constant learning. "I see the [progress of the] winery as writing a new recipe, finding the right ingredients," until it's right. The beauty of a tested recipe is that it gets passed on and each person who tries it adds their own flavor.

Last day of harvesting, late fall

Joseph D. Thomas

Buying and Serving Wine

Joseph D. Thomas

White grapes from Westport Rivers Vineyard

Reading a wine label can be confusing, so here are a few things to look for:

- *Estate means that all the wine in the bottle came from its own vineyard.*
- *A specific year on the label means that the juice that went into the wine was all from that year.*
- *Sulfites: wineries are required to list sulfites on the label. Sulfur is a naturally occurring organic substance that is completely harmless for most people. Some people, but very few, may have a mild to serious allergic reaction to it. Sulfur is not an artificial preservative, but it is sometimes sprayed on grapes to repel mildew or molds or is added in small amounts to white grape juice to prevent browning. Sulfites appear in many other foods such as packaged soups, dried fruit and processed meats.*

All wine is best stored on its side at 58°–64°. Sparkling wine made traditionally means it is fermented and handled like classic French Champagne. It should be set in ice for about 30 minutes, and served in a flute or tulip glass. If you've never done it, visit one of our local wineries (just as you would a farmstand) for a tour and tasting. What you learn from a 30-minute tour will change the way you enjoy your next glass of wine.

Pairing wine and foods is another way to increase the value you have sharing a bottle of wine. The good news is there are no hard and fast rules. If you don't care for the combination you've chosen, set your wine aside until you've finished eating, then enjoy your wine. Also, talk to the wine person at your liquor store and ask their advice. My brother Ian is in the business and loves to talk to his customers about wines, rising to the challenge of connecting people to the right wines. Establish what your likes and dislikes are, and how much you are willing to spend, then be flexible within your parameters.

Wines at the Sakonnet Vineyards' store in Little Compton

Joseph D. Thomas

Vinaigrette and Marinade

Verjus is the freshly pressed juice from underripe grapes (see description page 31). I use it in place of vinegar, lemon, lime or cooking wine, in everything from baking, to sauces, to a refreshing drink. Westport Rivers bottles and sells their own. This can be used as a marinade for vegetables, fish, beef and chicken.

In a small bowl, whisk together the verjus and salt to dissolve, then whisk in or shake in the oil. Toss over a green, pasta, or potato salad. Store leftovers in the refrigerator. Variation: Add 2 teaspoons chopped fresh herbs, chopped ginger or garlic and freshly ground black pepper. Store leftovers in a covered container in the refrigerator.

⅓ cup verjus, or "green juice" (see note)
¼ tsp. salt
½ cup oil (olive, canola, etc.)

Wine aging in oak barrels at Sakonnet Vineyards

Savory Verjus Rub for Chicken, Beef or Pork

Combine the spices, garlic, cilantro and verjus. Let steep about 10 minutes. Beat mixture into the softened butter a little at a time with a wooden spoon. Store in the refrigerator for up to 3 days. Can be frozen for several weeks.

To use: Bring the rub to room temperature and massage the rub into the meat for several minutes. The meat can be grilled, braised, roasted, or sautéed immediately or allowed to marinate for 1 day.

MAKES ENOUGH FOR 5 LBS. OF MEAT.

1 tsp. ground coriander
1 tbsp. chopped garlic
2 tsp. ground cumin
Pinch saffron threads
1 tbsp. chopped cilantro
½ cup verjus
6 tbsp. butter, softened

Bottles of verjus from Westport Rivers Vineyard and Winery

John K. Robson

Grilled Flank Steak with Mushrooms

1½–2 lbs. flank steak
Salt and pepper
Cooking oil
2 shallots, or 1 small onion and 1
 clove garlic, thinly sliced
1 lb. button or crimini
 mushrooms, trimmed and
 sliced in ¼" slices
⅓ cup crisp New England
 chardonnay
2 tbsp. chopped fresh basil
2 tsp. extra virgin olive oil or
 unsalted butter

The beauty of a cool-climate chardonnay is its versatility. Grilled beef may seem an unconventional dish to serve alongside, but it works. A salad tossed with a delicate vinaigrette of olive oil and verjus and a fresh bread will make this a meal.

Prepare the grill. When the coals are ready, season the meat with salt and pepper and brush with oil. Grill the meat on both sides to preferred temperature. Rest on a cooler portion of the grill. Set a sauté pan on the grill grate with one tablespoon cooking oil. Heat thoroughly, add the shallots and then cook until softened. Add the mushrooms and sprinkle with salt. Cook until they release and then reabsorb their juices. Pull the pan off the heat, pour in the wine and return it to the grill. Cook the wine down almost completely, stir in the basil and oil or butter and season to taste with salt. Hold warm. Slice the steak very thinly against the grain, transfer to a serving dish and spoon the mushrooms over the top.

MAKES 4 SERVINGS.

Autumn Vegetable Soup

4 tbsp. vegetable oil
1 small yellow onion, peeled and
 sliced
2 cloves garlic
1 medium russet potato, peeled,
 ½" dice
3 cups squash (butternut or
 acorn), peeled, 1" dice
2 carrots, peeled and sliced
1 macomber turnip, peeled, 1" dice
½ cup dry chardonnay
Water
8 fresh sage leaves
Salt and black pepper

GARNISH:
Sour cream
Sliced green onions
Fresh ground black pepper

In a 1½-gallon soup pot, heat the oil over medium heat, then slowly "sweat" the garlic and onion in the hot oil until the onions are limp and the garlic is fragrant. Add the squash and potato and cook until they begin to soften. Add the carrot and macomber and do the same. Pour in the wine and raise the heat to medium-high and allow the wine to simmer. Add water to just cover the vegetables, bring it up to a boil, then lower the heat so the soup is simmering and throw in the sage leaves. Cook until all the vegetables are tender, about 20–30 minutes. Cool to room temperature, then blend the soup in a blender in batches on low speed until completely smooth. Season to taste with salt and pepper.

Serve in a soup plate with a dollop of sour cream sprinkled with sliced green onions and a turn of fresh ground black pepper, and accompanied by a cool glass of a dry crisp chardonnay. We recommend hunks of buttered crusty bread to balance out this simple hearty repast for a chilly evening.

Roast Turkey
with Rosemary Scented Stuffing

Here, wine is used to season and moisten the stuffing.

Preheat oven to 425°. Place the crumbs, rosemary and garlic in a food processor with the chopping blade and pulse until the rosemary and garlic are in tiny pieces and thoroughly incorporated into the bread crumbs, then dump the mixture into a small mixing bowl. Drop the onion and dried fruit into the food processor and pulse-chop to small bits, then add to the mixing bowl of crumbs. Stir in the seasonings and wine and combine completely. Set the stuffing aside. Place the turkey skin side down on a cutting board, the narrow end pointing toward you. Fold the tender out over the nearest edge, then, with a thin sharp knife, slice a flap from top to bottom, from the center out toward the edge opposite the tender. (The breast can be ordered "butterflied" from a butcher to save time.) Open the meat up and spread the stuffing in the center leaving a small border around the edges. Fold the tender back over, then the cut-side can be folded over that. Tuck any extraneous meat or skin in and turn the whole shebang into a small glass baking dish so its skin side is up. Rub the skin with the brown sugar and season with salt and pepper. Roast for 30 minutes, then turn the oven down to 350° and cook for 45 minutes to an hour until completely cooked. Allow to sit at room temperature for at least 15 minutes before slicing. Leftovers can be held chilled for several days if tightly wrapped. Serving suggestions: Unsweetened applesauce slightly warmed complements the stuffing nicely and buttered rice or delicately seasoned mashed potatoes and steamed broccoli or late-season corn make a rounded meal.

MAKES 4–6 SERVINGS.

FOR THE STUFFING:
1 cup bread crumbs
1 clove garlic
1 tsp. fresh rosemary leaves
1 small yellow onion, peeled and quartered
¼ cup dried apple or apricot, slivered
¼ cup Johannisberg Riesling
6 turns on a mill or a generous pinch black pepper
¼ tsp. salt

FOR THE TURKEY:
2–3 lb. boneless turkey breast, skin and tender on
1 tsp. brown sugar
Salt and black pepper

Harvesting white grapes at Westport Rivers Vineyard

John K. Robson

Sparkling Fondue

1 tbsp. cornstarch
2 tsp. verjus, or lemon juice
1 cup sparkling wine
¾ lb. Gruyere cheese, grated
¾ lb. Swiss cheese, grated
½ tsp. fresh thyme leaves, or
    ¼ cup sliced Greek or Sicilian
    olives, well drained, or
    Pinch of ground nutmeg and
    cayenne pepper

Served with a tossed salad, this will make a full meal for four. I have served the fondue with thyme paired with blanc de blancs. The olive and spicy versions would do well with a brut or blanc de noir.

Stir the verjus into the cornstarch, then stir in the wine. Combine all ingredients in a heavy-bottomed stainless pan or fondue pot. Heat on low for 8–12 minutes until melted, stirring occasionally. Be careful not to overheat or the cheese will toughen. The texture should be liquid and the cheese should have an easy give and a soft stretch. Serve immediately with sliced fresh bread or toasted baguettes.

A Sparkling Snack

GARLIC AND PARMESAN PITA CHIPS
¼ cup canola oil
1 tsp. chopped garlic
3 pita pockets
½ cup grated parmesan cheese

A good Sparkling wine can make any day special. Sharing a bottle with your friends doesn't mean shopping for unusual foods to serve. Try shopping in your cupboards first. Some snack ideas to serve with a blanc de noir or brut sparkler:

- *Garlic and Parmesan Pita Chips*
- *Spanish or black olives, drained and tossed with chopped parsley, olive oil and crushed red pepper*
- *Dry roasted peanuts seasoned with cayenne pepper and a squeeze of lime*
- *Sardines in oil served on toasted English muffin wedges and sprinkled with chopped fresh thyme or chives*
- *Grilled ham and Swiss cheese sandwiches with spicy coarse mustard.*

GARLIC AND PARMESAN PITA CHIPS
Preheat oven to 425°. Heat the oil and garlic over a low flame until the smell of garlic reaches your nose, then remove from the heat. Cut the pita into 8 triangles and pull apart at the seam (16 large chips per pita). Place the triangles inside-up on a cookie sheet and brush each one with the garlic oil then sprinkle with parmesan. Bake until browned, about 7 minutes. Cool and serve. Store leftovers in an airtight container.

Westport Rivers sparkling wines

John K. Robson

A Taste of Pear and Blue Cheese

Really a dressed-up pizza, a medium-to-full-bodied red, or even a late-harvest riesling or botrytised wine like sauternes is recommended to accompany.

Note: Pat Fonseca of Spring Valley Water recommends using natural spring water for yeast doughs (as well as brewing coffee and tea). Chlorine is a yeast killer and is unpleasant to taste.

In a bowl, combine the water, wine, honey, yeast, salt and butter. Stir well. Dump in the flour and combine, using a wooden spoon until thoroughly incorporated and the dough forms a ball and does not stick to your fingers. Add more flour as needed. Pour about 1 tablespoon canola oil into the bottom of a 2-quart bowl, drop in the dough and roll it around to coat it entirely. Cover the bowl with a damp cloth or plastic wrap and set in a warm spot. Allow the dough to rise until doubled. Preheat oven to 450°. Spray or lightly oil two cookie sheets. Dump the dough out onto a floured surface, cut it into four equal parts, and roll each into a free-form circle about ⅓" thick (precision is not important here), and lay them out on the pans. Brush each with butter, set the pears in a single layer next, then top with crumbled cheese. Sprinkle each with sage and nuts, then bake for 10–12 minutes until the crust is golden. Let them sit at room temperature for several minutes. Transfer to a large cutting board and cut them into wedges. Serve as a passed hors d'oeuvre or plated with a small salad of butter lettuce lightly tossed with olive oil and salt.

MAKES 4 LARGE OR 8 SMALL APPETIZERS.

FOR THE CRUST:
- ¾ cup water, body temperature
- ¼ cup white wine
- 2 tsp. active dry yeast
- 2 tsp. honey
- 1 tsp. salt
- 1 tbsp. butter, melted
- 2 cups unbleached flour

ON TOP:
- 2 oz. butter, melted
- 4 pears, peeled, halved, cored and thinly sliced
- 12 oz. blue-veined cheese (blue, saga or both) I use Great Hill Blue, made in Marion, MA.
- 2 tsp. chopped fresh sage leaves
- 2 tbsp. finely chopped walnuts (optional)

John K. Robson

Sakonnet Vineyards

Verjus and Onion Sauce

This versatile sauce can be served warm or at room temperature with steak, fish, shrimp, poultry or pork, whether grilled, roasted, sautéed or baked.

In a sauté pan, heat the oil over a medium-low heat until hot, and stir in the onions and garlic. Cook the onions slowly until they collapse, and then begin to brown lightly. Turn up the heat to medium-high, pour in the verjus, bring to a low boil and reduce the liquid down by half. Pour in the stock, bring to a low boil and reduce the liquid until it thickens, almost coating the onions. Remove from the heat and season with salt, chives and herbs. Serve warm or at room temperature.

MAKES ABOUT 1½ CUPS OF SAUCE.

- 1 tbsp. canola oil
- 1 med. yellow onion, peeled, cut in half and thinly sliced
- 1 med. red onion, peeled, cut in half and thinly sliced
- 1 clove garlic, peeled and sliced
- ½ cup verjus
- ½ cup chicken, beef or fish stock
- ½ tsp. salt
- 2 tbsp. chopped chives
- 1 tbsp. chopped rosemary, parsley, sage or thyme

Summer Pasta with Chardonnay

3 cloves garlic, peeled
1 small onion, peeled and
    quartered
1 med. zucchini, trimmed and cut
    into chunks
½ cup fresh basil leaves
¼ cup plus 3 tbsp olive oil
¼ cup chardonnay
8 roma or plum tomatoes,
    seeded and chopped, or 1
    28-oz. can whole tomatoes,
    drained and chopped
½ tsp. salt plus more to taste
¼ tsp. sugar
1 lb. pasta (fusilli or spaghetti)
6 oz. mozzarella cheese, cubed
Freshly ground black pepper to
    taste

The vegetables are first macerated (softened) in the wine before they are cooked. The resulting flavor is bright but well married.

Combine the garlic, onion, zucchini and basil in the bowl of a food processor fitted with a steel blade. Pulse until ingredients are coarsely chopped, about 30 seconds. Scrape the vegetables into a large mixing bowl and stir in ¼ cup of the olive oil, the chardonnay, tomatoes, salt and sugar. Set aside.

Bring a large pot of salted water to a rolling boil. Add the pasta and cook until tender. Drain, return to the pot, and toss with the remaining 3 tablespoons of olive oil. Place a large skillet over medium-high heat for 1 to 2 minutes until it is very hot. Pour the contents of the mixing bowl into the skillet and stir. Simmer for 8–10 minutes, or until the onion has lost its pungency. Remove from heat and pour over the cooked pasta. Add the cheese, and season with salt and pepper. Serve immediately.

MAKES 4–6 SERVINGS.

Grilled Salmon with Corn Salsa

FOR THE SALMON:
4 4–6 oz. pieces boneless
    salmon fillets
½ cup dry Johannisberg Riesling
¼ cup canola or vegetable oil
Pinch ground black pepper
Pinch ground cumin
Salt

FOR THE SALSA:
2 ears corn, cooked
1 avocado, peeled and diced
1 small red onion, small dice
3 plum tomatoes, seeded and diced
1 cucumber, peeled, seeded and
    diced
2 tsp. chopped fresh cilantro
2 tbsp. olive or canola oil
1 tbsp. lemon juice or riesling
Pinch salt
2 jalapeños, finely minced
    (optional)

FOR THE SALMON:
Place the salmon in a glass pie or baking dish. In a small mixing bowl, combine the wine, oil, pepper and cumin and whisk thoroughly. Pour the mixture over the fish and allow to marinate in the refrigerator about an hour. Remove the salmon from the dish and discard the marinade. Season the fish with salt and grill over hot coals on a grill grate sprayed with non-stick cooking spray. Cook the fish on both sides for 2–3 minutes per side until the center is firm, but not flaky. Serve with a generous spoonful of salsa over the top and a fresh green salad.

FOR THE SALSA:
Cut the corn kernels off the cob. Toss them in a mixing bowl with the remaining ingredients and leave covered at room temperature until serving. Check the flavor and adjust the salt to your taste. The salsa can be made a day in advance, stored covered in the refrigerator, and the leftovers can be stored the same way for three days.

MAKES 4 SERVINGS.

Robust Curry Stew

This recipe shakes up holiday leftovers with the exotic flavor of curry. If you like spicy, turn up the heat by adding more cayenne or a couple of hot peppers. Serve over egg noodles, rice or couscous. A fruity, perfumed riesling or gewurztraminer would be ideal to pair with this dish. A rich off-dry blush is also an option.

Combine the oil, garlic and curry in the bottom of a cold stew pot and set over low heat. Cook slowly until the curry and garlic reach your nose, then turn up the heat to medium. Pour in the wine, add the cayenne and simmer until the wine reduces down by half in volume. Add the onions, with any raw vegetables, and cook, stirring occasionally, for about 5 minutes. Raise the heat to medium-high, add the stock and bring to a boil, then lower the heat so that the liquid is simmering and stir in the remaining vegetables, apples and meat. Simmer until all the vegetables are softened, almost collapsed, and stir in the potatoes. Cook for 10 to 15 minutes or until the liquid has thickened. Season to taste with salt and pepper. Serving suggestion: sprinkle toasted almonds and dried currants or raisins over the top, or set out the cranberry sauce...again!

MAKES 4 SERVINGS.

4 cloves garlic
3 tbsp. canola or vegetable oil
2½ tsp. curry powder
½ cup off-dry blush or white wine
¼ tsp. cayenne pepper
2 yellow onions, chopped
4 cups raw or cooked vegetables (butternut squash, carrots, zucchini, turnip, mushrooms, eggplant, etc.), separate the raw and cooked vegetables
2 cups stock or water
2 firm apples, peeled, cored and diced. (macoun or granny smith)
2 cups cooked meat or poultry (diced ham, chicken, turkey, lamb, beef or pork)
1½ cups mashed potatoes, or 1 cup potato flakes
Salt and pepper

Pruned vines at Sakonnet Vineyards

Joseph D. Thomas

Riesling Cake

½ cup finely ground almonds
½ cup riesling
⅓ cup honey
4 oz. sweet butter
⅓ cup light brown sugar
2 large eggs
2 cups all-purpose flour
2 tsp. baking powder
Pinch salt

The aroma of this cake baking is mouth watering. Enjoy.

Preheat oven to 350°. Spray or butter a bundt pan generously and dust with the ground almonds. Set aside. Warm the riesling in a small saucepan over a low flame. Stir in the honey, remove from heat and cool to room temperature. Cream the butter and the brown sugar until light. Add the eggs one at a time and incorporate completely. Sift together the flour, salt and baking powder in a separate bowl. Add the flour and the riesling syrup in thirds, alternately, to the butter mixture. Fill the pan and bake 30–35 minutes until golden and completely set. Cool 1 hour before unmolding.

Serving suggestion: Unmold the cake onto sweetened whipped cream, dust the top with powdered sugar and garnish with red and golden raspberries.

Makes 1 bundt cake.

Westport Rivers Vineyard

John K. Robson

Antique hand press at Sakonnet Vineyards

Joseph D. Thomas

Smooth Wine Cheesecake

Pair this simple cheesecake with a rich, fruity white dessert wine or lightly sweet sparkling wine.

6 oz. softened cream cheese
⅓ cup sugar
3 eggs, room temperature
¼ cup eiswein, late harvest riesling, or white dessert wine
1 cup half-and-half

Preheat oven to 325°. Beat the cream cheese on medium-high speed until fluffy. Beat in the sugar on low, then beat until fluffy on medium-high. Beat the eggs in on low one at a time. Stream in the wine, then the half-and-half. Pour into a buttered or sprayed 9" cake pan. Set the cake pan into a deep roasting pan, fill with warm water until the level reaches halfway up the cake pan. Slide into the oven and cook until just set in the center, about 1 hour. Cool on a rack completely and chill. The cheesecake can be sliced or spooned out of the pan and served with fresh peach slices or sautéed apples.

MAKES ONE 9" CAKE PAN.

Joseph D. Thomas

Red Wine Biscotti

These are not too hard but are a nice texture for dunking in coffee, tea or a glass of wine!

2 sticks butter, softened
1½ cups granulated sugar
3 large eggs
3 tbsp. red wine (fruity, dry)
1 tsp. vanilla
4 cups unbleached flour
1 tbsp. baking powder
½ tsp. salt
1 cup roughly chopped walnuts

Beat the butter with an electric mixer until light. Stream in the sugar and beat until fluffy. Beat in the eggs on medium speed one at a time until thoroughly incorporated. Beat in the wine and vanilla. In a separate bowl, stir together the flour, salt and baking powder. Fold the flour mixture into the butter and sugar mixture in 3 additions. Fold in the nuts. Cover the dough and chill for 30 minutes.

Preheat the oven to 350°. Lightly spray or line 2 cookie sheets with parchment. Split half of the dough onto each cookie sheet and shape into rectangular loaves. Bake for 20–30 minutes, until lightly golden. Cool completely. Slice using a serrated knife into ½"–¾" slices.

Raise the oven temperature to 425°. Lay the slices flat on the cookie sheets and toast each side for 5–8 minutes until golden. Cool on a rack and store in an airtight container.

MAKES 4 DOZEN.

Pinot noir and chardonnay (top) grapes ready for harvest at Westport Rivers Vineyards

John K. Robson

CHAPTER SEVEN

The Westport Macomber

*For laborers, if those that sow…turnips, carrots, cabbage and the
like and give yearly for an acre of land…better or at least as
good ground may be had and cost nothing but labor.* —Captain John
Smith, presenting his case for colonization, *New England's Trials*, 1614

The story of the Westport macomber reflects the history of America itself: People of faith packing up their families, their few possessions and boarding ships, hoping to create a new life in a place they have seen only in the imagination. What courage that must have taken! In my life of relative ease and comfort, I have given into moments of ungratefulness and downright complaining, as have we all. I was struck by the foolishness of my behavior as I read William Bradford's account of his first year here, watching half of his new countrymen die. Yet he held on to his faith in God and never gave up.

George Smith of Noquochoke Orchards shows off his prize-winning Westport macomber—a cross of a radish, turnip and cabbage.

John K. Robson

I was equally in awe as I read about William Maycomber (Macomber) and his family William Macomber was born in Inverness, Scotland in 1610. He and his two brothers arrived in the Plymouth Colony before 1638. The first mention of William in the Plymouth Colony Records was April 2, 1638, which stated that he had served his apprenticeship as a cooper. The August 3, 1640 entry states that he was granted wood for his coopery. The next reference to William came after his move to Marshfield, where he was fined for "speaking to the Indians."

During these years, William Macomber married Ursilla and together they had eight children. Their son William was born in 1655, around his father's 45th birthday. He later married Mary and purchased a 140-plus-acre farm in the Westport portion of old Dartmouth.

Six generations passed and the farm remained in the family and grew to 500 acres. Israel Macomber and his wife Mary E. Tripp Manchester had four boys and enjoyed a life of devotion to each other and their children. "For nearly half a century, this good couple walked hand in hand bringing up their children to maturity and an honorable position in life, and have the satisfaction of knowing none are recreant to the principles inculcated by their ancestors." The two eldest, William and Isaac, married and left the farm, both seeking some adventure in California before returning home to settle near the family farm. The younger, Adin and Elihu, never married and remained on the farm with their parents. They were ambitious, hard-working farmers who loved their family and the land.

Elihu Macomber with his cousin (center) and an unidentified man

The turnip arrived in the Massachusetts Bay Colony in 1629. The new residents of the farming-based colonies raised the turnip in abundance as it was hearty against cold weather, stored beautifully throughout the winter, and was inexpensive to farm. These gentleman farmers, Adin and Elihu Macomber, also cultivated turnips. The two men returned from a fair in Philadelphia in 1876 with seeds for experimentation—planting radishes next to rutabagas (a 17th-century crossbreed of a cabbage and a turnip) to allow for cross-pollination. The Westport macomber was born. Like a 6-foot, blue-eyed, olive-skinned child of 5'5" parents of Nordic and Iberian ancestry, the Westport macomber, commonly called the macomber turnip, inherited the white flesh of its radish parent and

Elihu and daughter Mildred Howland

cruciferae Brassica Rapa (turnip) grandparent, but an unusual sweetness and horseradish aroma, raw and cooked. The Macomber men, obviously pleased with the resulting vegetable, continued to produce seeds and sold them to their neighbors quite possibly until their deaths. Adin died at 70 in 1915, Elihu at 86 in 1933.

In the decade Elihu died, almost every farm in the region was growing turnips, but only four or five Westport farms held the original macomber seed. The Cape White and Bristol White varieties were the most prolific. The persona of the turnip was becoming less than glamorous. However, its abundance kept the price low, making it the staple food of the poor and winter fare for livestock. "Turnip Chewer" was the name given to those of meager means.

Despite low public opinion, several families held onto the seed and understood its local importance. The Boans in Westport are one such family. A quote from Westport farmer John Boan in a September 1988 *Boston Magazine* article states, "A macomber can grow up to eight pounds, but people (now) like them small. They used to like them large in the old days—not so many to peel." Perhaps this is the reason the Macomber brothers developed the vegetable! It has been my experience with the Westport macomber that, small or large, the taste is sweet and smooth.

What about the Macomber family? Mrs. Theresa Frances Macomber Gifford, born in 1910, lives on the remaining 40 acres of farmland. Her father Nason Robinson and mother Kate Cornell were vegetable farmers who made the regular

Elihu's account ledger showing prices and quantities, 1899

trek to Fall River to sell their cabbages and family white-fleshed rutabaga. Nason eventually turned a good portion of his land over to ice ponds, selling and delivering directly to businesses and homes.

Mrs. Gifford remembers her mother's cooking as very simple and hearty. "She only had a few recipes that she knew by heart. We always ate the (macomber) turnip boiled and mashed with butter." How accurate could a recipe be when cooking on a woodstove with no thermostat or flame control? When baking a cake, Kate would "…put her hand in the oven to tell if it was right." Those were days of hard work but happy ones for Theresa.

After she married, the Giffords lived in the Macomber family home. Son Howard Gifford, also a Westport resident, recalls raising chickens and cows, selling milk and eggs in his youth to make money during wartime. Howard did not choose farming as his life's work. "At 16, I had a car and I wanted to just go!" The world of the

Ron Rolo, Standard-Times

Al Lees displays his macomber in 1987.

farmer seemed to have too many limits. Looking back, though, Howard has fond and good memories of his young life on the Macomber farm.

The Westport macomber today is making a strong comeback. Over the last decade, efforts by farmers like the Boan family and others who have held onto the original seed and, more recently, efforts of the Coastal Growers Association have catapulted the vegetable to star status. When they are ready for harvest, most crops are sold before they are pulled out of the ground. Demand from large and gourmet grocers, as well as the region's best restaurants, grows annually. The goal of Coastal Growers Association is to make the macomber to Westport what the onion is to Vidalia, Georgia, a unique and successful agricultural product synonymous with the region.

Growing the Westport macomber is an eight-month-long proposition, beginning in April. Taproot from the previous harvest is planted. A blossoming stem grows and matures until June when the seeds are harvested. The seeds are dried for a month or so and planted. Harvest is in October or November.

The macomber is a versatile vegetable, delicious in so many ways and appears in so many dishes. The health benefits of the macomber mirror those of most cruciferous vegetables: high fiber, no fat, loaded with calcium, vitamin C, carotene, potassium and iron. It doesn't get better than this.

A group gathers annually in Westport to celebrate their favorite son, William Macomber. They cook dishes with the white rutabaga that range from the traditional mash, to the unusual pie, to the downright outrageous *Macomber Coladas* recipe (not included— you'll have to experiment for yourself!). Some of the following recipes were collected from the six Annual Macomber Dinners while others were offered by area chefs who look forward to harvest season and a favored local ingredient.

Buying a Macomber

The macomber should be solid and fairly dense-feeling. Sometimes the greens are left on top. The vegetable should be washed and peeled before boiling. Look for them starting in October. It is said they are best after the first frost.

Warm Westport Macomber Salad

1 medium Westport Macomber
1 small onion
1 stalk celery
1 clove garlic
4 slices bacon
⅓ cup dry white wine
⅓ cup olive oil
Salt and pepper to taste

Anonymous contribution to the macomber dinner.

Peel and cube macomber. Cook in salted water until just tender. Hold warm. Chop onion, celery and garlic together and spread over the bottom of a glass microwaveable 8" x 12" dish. Lay bacon on top of the mixture and cover with a paper towel. Microwave on high for 5 minutes and allow to stand for 5 minutes. Chop bacon into small pieces. Drain macomber and mix with the above ingredients. Combine the wine and olive oil and add seasonings. Pour over macomber and stir well. Cover with plastic wrap and microwave for up to 3 minutes. Rotate once while cooking. Serve immediately.

MAKES 4–6 SIDE DISHES.

Carrots Macomber Mash

1 lb. Macomber turnip, peeled and cut in ¾" chunks
1 lb. carrots, peeled and cut in ¾" chunks
Salt and pepper

Simmer both separately in lightly salted water that is level with the vegetables over medium heat until tender. Drain over a bowl, saving some of the cooking liquid. Mash together by hand or with an electric mixer. Stir in cooking liquid if desired if the mash is too thick. Season with salt and pepper to taste, and add butter if you wish. Save the remaining cooking liquid to add to a soup. It will keep refrigerated for 2 or 3 days.

MAKES ABOUT 3 CUPS.

Coastal Growers Association, Westport, MA

Note: This recipe has been a common one in so many homes and restaurant kitchens in Westport, I am not sure one person or group can lay claim to it.

Westport Macomber
and Two Potato Gratin

Stephen serves this at an annual fund-raising dinner. I have been told by many that they return to this dinner every year not only to support the cause but to get a taste of this dish!

Preheat oven to 400°. In a 5-quart pot, gently sweat the leeks and onions in butter over medium heat until softened. Stir in potatoes and macomber until coated with butter. Pour in the stock and cream, raise the heat to medium-high and simmer until the potatoes are just tender. Remove from heat. Season to taste with salt. In a mixing bowl, combine the crumbs and half of the cheeses. In a buttered casserole dish, alternate the potatoes and macomber with the cheeses in two layers, then sprinkle the crumb mix over the top. Bake until browned, about 15–20 minutes.

MAKES ABOUT ONE LARGE DEEP ROASTING PAN OR 3–4-QUART CASSEROLE.

Stephen Worden, Worden's 7 Water Street Restaurant, Dartmouth

1 leek, washed, chopped and drained
2 med. onions, peeled and chopped
2 tbsp. butter
3 sweet potatoes, peeled and cut in ¾" dice
3 russet potatoes, peeled and cut in ¾" dice
2 med. macombers peeled and cut in ¾" dice
1 qt. heavy cream
2 cups chicken broth or water
Salt
2 cups cheddar cheese, grated
1 cup parmesan cheese, grated
1 cup bread crumbs

Bisque of Roots, Leeks and Apples

Simmer the macomber, rutabaga and potatoes in a 2-gallon pot in stock until tender. In a separate pan sauté the leeks and apples in 4–6 tablespoons butter until tender. Stir into simmered veggies. Purée all cooked ingredients and stock in batches, adding salt, white pepper and remaining butter to taste. Add jalapeño tabasco sauce and curry to taste. Return to heat, add cream just before serving and top each serving with ½ teaspoon of chives.

MAKES 1½ GALLONS.

Betse V. Downey, Dartmouth, MA

8 cups Westport Macomber, peeled and cut in large cubes
4 cups rutabaga, peeled and cut in large cubes
3 medium russet potatoes, peeled and large dice
4 qts. vegetable, chicken or turkey stock
5 med. or 3 large leeks, washed and sliced thinly
4 apples (2 sweet and 2 tart), cored and sliced
8 tbsp. butter
1 pt. light or heavy cream
1½ oz. jalapeño tabasco sauce
1½ tbsp. mild Indian curry
Salt
White pepper
Chives, chopped fine for topping

The Oakdale Farm in Rehoboth

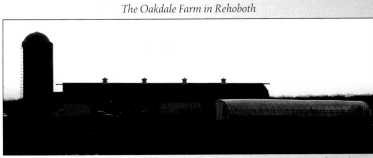

Joseph D. Thomas

Linguine Florentine á la Macomber

1 Westport Macomber, cut in
    eight pieces
4–5 cloves garlic, peeled
3 tbsp. unsalted butter
Salt and pepper
1 large onion, coarsely chopped
3 tsp. canola oil
10 oz. fresh spinach, washed
1 whole nutmeg
1 oz. light cream
3–4 fresh basil leaves
1 lb. pasta (linguine or fettucine)

Simmer together macomber and garlic until macomber is soft. Drain. Save the cooking liquid for soup. Purée in a blender with 1 tablespoon of butter and a *small* amount of macomber stock to a thick sauce. Season with salt and keep warm. In a wok or deep sauté pan, sweat chopped onion in 1 tablespoon of butter and all the canola oil until translucent and beginning to color. Wilt spinach on top of onions, combining well, and season with salt, pepper and a few grates of nutmeg. Purée or finely chop spinach and onions in a blender with 1 tablespoon of butter, light cream and fresh basil leaves. Keep warm. Cook and drain pasta. Combine sauces and pasta and serve immediately, or serve pasta on a large platter and alternate ribbons of sauce, keeping the green and white separate. Serve as a side dish with fish or chicken.

MAKES 4–6 SERVINGS.

Betse V. Downey, Dartmouth, MA

Simple Mashed Macomber

1 Westport Macomber
Water
Salt
Butter

This preparation was most common to our early area residents. The delicate and sweet texture and flavor of the Westport macomber requires very little to enhance it.

Peel and cut the macomber into 1" dice. Place into a pot with water up to the level of the vegetable. Toss in 1 teaspoon salt, cover and bring to a boil on high heat. Lower the flame to medium and simmer until tender. At this point the macomber can be mashed with a hand masher or puréed in a food processor or blender with the liquid. If the purée is loose or watery, return to a medium-low heat and slowly cook off some of the liquid, stirring occasionally. Season to taste with salt and a little butter. Any leftovers can be refrigerated and used to thicken a soup or add a special taste to mashed potatoes.

YIELD DEPENDS ON SIZE.

Flowers for sale at George Farm

John K. Robson

Savory Macomber Spoon Bread

A sweeter version of this same spoon bread can be found in the Apple and Peach chapter. This is a creamy, flavorful side dish that adds a touch of elegance to an any-night-of-the-week dinner.

Place the purée ingredients in a 2-quart covered saucepan, bring to boil. Simmer until tender, about 15 minutes. Pour the contents of the pan into a bar blender or food processor and blend until completely smooth (this step may require two batches). Pour the purée into a deep skillet and cook over low flame until all excess water has evaporated. Yields about 3 cups.

Preheat oven to 375° and butter a 2-quart soufflé dish. In a saucepan heat the half-and-half, butter, honey, and salt until hot and the butter has melted. Stir in the cornmeal and cook over a low flame, stirring continuously, until thickened. Transfer the cornmeal mush to a large mixing bowl and allow to cool for several minutes, stirring occasionally. Stir in the macomber purée, baking powder, and pepper, then add the egg yolks and stir until combined thoroughly. In a separate bowl, beat the egg whites briskly until soft peaks form, then fold into the spoon bread base in two additions using large, gentle strokes with a rubber spatula. Transfer to the prepared soufflé dish and bake until golden brown and puffed through the center, about 30–35 minutes. The spoon bread is best served warm. The remaining macomber purée can be used in soup, chowder, or as is with any meat or fish instead of potatoes.

MAKES ONE 2-QUART SOUFFLÉ DISH.

THE PURÉE:
4 cups macombers, peeled and large dice
2 tart baking apples, peeled and large dice
1 yellow onion, peeled and chopped
3 cups water
1 tsp. salt

THE CORNMEAL MUSH:
2 cups half-and-half
3 tbsp. unsalted butter
1 tsp. honey
1 tsp. salt
1 cup johnnycake or cornmeal
1 cup macomber/apple puree
1 tsp. baking powder
6 turns freshly ground pepper
5 eggs separated

John K. Robson

Macomber & Carrot Sunflower Muffins

This is Shirley's macomber dinner contribution.

Preheat oven to 350°. In mixing bowl or food processor, combine the eggs, honey, oil, milk or yogurt and vanilla. In another bowl, combine the pastry flour, wheat germ, oat bran and baking powder. Grease 12 regular sized muffin cups or line with foil or paper baking cups. Combine the two mixtures. Stir in macomber, carrot and sunflower seeds. Spoon batter into the muffin cups and bake for about 20 minutes. A toothpick inserted in the center should come out clean.

MAKES 12 MUFFINS.

Shirley Mae Robbins, Paradise Hill Farm, Westport, MA

2 eggs
¼ cup honey
2 tbsp. softened unsalted butter or olive oil
1 cup soy milk, buttermilk or yogurt
1 tsp. vanilla
2 tbsp. wheat germ
1 cup sifted whole wheat pastry flour
2 tbsp. oat bran
2 tsp. baking powder
1 cup shredded macomber
½ cup shredded carrot
½ cup sunflower seeds

Smoky Chicken, Corn and Westport Macomber Chowder

5 ears corn on the cob
3 cups macombers, diced ½"
1 qt. chicken stock
2 cups sweet potato, diced ½"
1½ cups red bliss potato, diced ½"
¼ cup canola or corn oil
1½ cups onions, diced ½"
1 cup green peppers, diced ½"
1 cup red peppers, diced ½"
¾ cup celery, diced ½"
1 jalapeño pepper, finely minced
3 cloves garlic, minced
1 lb. chicken breast, diced ½"
1 tsp. thyme leaves
1 tbsp. parsley, chopped
1 tbsp. Worcestershire sauce
2 tsp. liquid smoke
2 cups heavy or light cream
Salt and pepper to taste

Boil corn, cool and remove kernels from the cob. Boil 1½ cups macombers in 1 cup water, purée, and reserve to thicken soup. In stock pot, heat chicken stock to boil. Add sweet potato, bliss potato and remaining Macomber. Boil 2 minutes. Reduce to a simmer. Heat half the oil in sauté pan. Sauté onions, peppers and celery. Add jalapeño pepper and garlic. Cook until the vegetables are soft and translucent, then stir into the soup. Place the pan back over medium-high heat with the other half of the oil. When the oil is hot, sauté chicken breast until golden, then add to soup. Add thyme, parsley, Worcestershire, and smoke, then simmer about 30 minutes. Add cream and season to taste with salt and pepper.

MAKES APPROXIMATELY 1 GALLON.

Michael Frady, Chef, The Barn, Adamsville, RI

Westport Macomber Cake

¾ cup brown sugar
1¼ cups sugar
1½ cups oil
3 eggs
2 tsp. vanilla
2¼ cups flour
2 tsp. cinnamon
2 tsp. baking soda
1 tsp. salt
2 cups grated macombers
1½ cups shredded coconut
1 cup chopped walnuts
1 8-oz. can crushed pineapple

FROSTING:
8 oz. cream cheese
¼ cup milk
¼ tsp. salt
½ cup softened butter
2 tsp. vanilla
3½ cups sifted powdered sugar

This cake is dark, rich and very moist.

Preheat oven to 350°. Combine sugars, oil, eggs and vanilla. Sift together flour, cinnamon, baking soda, and salt. Stir into the liquid mixture. Fold in coconut, macomber, walnuts and pineapple. Pour into a greased 9" x 13" baking pan and bake for 50 minutes or until done.

FROSTING:
Beat the ingredients to proper consistency with a beater or food processor until smooth. Frost cake when cooled.

MAKES 18–24 SERVINGS.

Hilare A. Downey, Dartmouth, MA

Pork with Macombers

This is a hometown recipe from a Louisiana-raised food lover. Both were common items raised on the family farms of South Louisiana. He replaces the traditional turnip in this family recipe with the Westport macomber.

Season the pork to taste with the salt, black and cayenne peppers. Heat the oil in the bottom of a 6-quart pot (cast iron is the pan of choice). Brown the pork chops in batches; do not overcrowd the pan. Set the browned chops on a plate to hold them.

With the pot on medium heat, stir the flour into the hot oil to make a "roux" (See page 49). Cook the mix until it turns dark brown. Keep it moving with a wooden spoon, being careful not to scorch it. Stir in the onion, garlic and peppers and cook until they soften. Slowly stir in the hot water or stock, raise the fire and bring it to a boil. Reduce the heat to a simmer. Add the pork, juices and all, to the pot and simmer for about 45 minutes, until the pork is tender. Add the diced macomber and cook for another 10-15 minutes until completely tender. Season with salt and pepper to taste. In a separate pan, render the bacon of its fat over medium heat. Remove the crispy pieces and hold. (macomber greens can be quickly sautéed in the bacon fat, if you were able to get them. Stir them into the pot.) Serve the pork and macomber over steamed rice topped with the crispy bacon.

MAKES 6–8 SERVINGS.

Michael Frady, Chef, The Barn, Adamsville, RI

3 lbs. pork chops, ½" thick
Salt
Black pepper
Cayenne pepper
½ cup oil
½ cup all-purpose flour
1 large onion, ½" dice
1 large green pepper, ½" dice
3 cloves garlic, minced
3–4 cups water or chicken stock, heated
4 medium Westport macombers, peeled and diced into ¾" cubes. If the greens accompany, wash them well and coarsely chop
8 strips bacon, cut in ½" pieces

Pickled Macomber

This is a delicious, unusual pickle somewhat resembling watermelon pickles. It keeps well in the refrigerator for several months and goes with any meats or poultry.

Cut macomber into ⅛" slices. Sprinkle with salt. Let stand 1½ hours. Drain thoroughly. Squeeze slices gently to remove brine. Put sugar, vinegar and paprika in saucepan. Bring to a boil. Add whole cloves or pickling spices. Add macomber slices. Bring to a boil again. Reduce heat and simmer 2 minutes. Cool, cover and refrigerate. Drain pickles to serve.

Tom Porter, Westport, MA

1 lb. Macomber
2 tbsp. salt
¾ cup sugar
1 cup white vinegar
1 tsp. paprika
1 tbsp. whole cloves or pickling spice

Portuguese Shepherd's Pie

For the Seasoned Beef:
3 lbs. ground sirloin
½ tsp. minced garlic
1 tsp. ground cumin seed
1 tbsp. chopped fresh basil
1 tsp. Portuguese allspice
1 tsp. ground black pepper
2 large eggs, beaten
¼ cup dry blush
1½ tsp salt

For the Pie:
1 28-oz. can crushed tomatoes
4 med. white potatoes, sliced thin
2 med. yellow onions, sliced thin
1 macomber, 1½-2 lbs., peeled
    and shredded
1 cup corn kernels

Place all the ingredients for the seasoned beef in a mixing bowl and combine thoroughly. Preheat oven to 350°. Spoon a thin even layer of crushed tomato over the bottom of the pan, followed by a slightly overlapped layer of sliced potatoes, then spread the onions, then add half the beef mix. Sprinkle half the shredded macomber and corn over the top. Repeat the process. Bake until it begins bubbling and is cooked in the center, about 45 minutes to 1 hour.

Makes one 13" x 9" dish (8–10 servings).

Marie Pray, Oakdale Farms, Rehoboth, MA

Macomber Ginger Pie

Ginger Snap Crust:
24 ginger snaps
¼ cup butter
2–3 tbsp. sugar

Filling:
2 eggs
1½ cups macomber mash (see
    below)
¾ cup sugar
¼ cup maple syrup
1 tsp. cinnamon
1 tsp. ground ginger
1 cup evaporated milk
¼ cup water
Pinch nutmeg

This pie fooled a crowd with its pumpkin-like flavor and texture.

Grind ginger snaps in a food processor into coarse crumbs. Add the butter and sugar and pulse until thoroughly combined. Press into a 9" pie plate evenly around the edge.

In a small bowl, beat eggs until light and set aside. Combine "mash" with sugar, syrup, cinnamon and ginger and stir until there are no lumps. Add eggs and blend. Add milk and water and mix well. Pour filling into shell and sprinkle with nutmeg. Bake at 400° for 15 minutes, then reduce temperature to 350° and bake for 45 minutes or until knife inserted in middle comes out clean. Cool completely before cutting.

Makes one 9" pie.

Macomber Mash

3 cups macomber
1½ cups diced carrots
¼ cup sour cream
¼ tsp. nutmeg
Salt

Peel and dice macomber. Cook with carrots in a small amount of water until soft. Drain and cool. Purée in food processor until smooth. Add sour cream, nutmeg and salt to taste. Blend. Use leftover mash for dinner or as soup base.

Makes about 3 cups.

John DeSouza, Massachusetts Specialty Food Association

Macomber Puff

Cook macomber until tender in a pot of salted water. Drain and mash. Add butter and eggs, beat well. (This could be done a day ahead.) Heat oven to 375°. Combine flour, sugar, baking powder, salt, pepper and nutmeg. Stir the macomber into the flour mixture, spread into 9"x13" glass dish. Stir the melted butter into the crumbs and sprinkle over the top. Bake for 25 minutes or until brown.

MAKES 6 SERVINGS.

Coastal Growers Association, Westport, MA

6 cups Macomber turnips,
  peeled and cubed
2 tbsp. butter
2 eggs, beaten
3 tbsp. flour
1 tbsp. brown sugar
1 tsp. baking powder
¾ tsp. salt
⅛ tsp. pepper
Pinch nutmeg
½ cup fine bread crumbs
2 tbsp. melted butter

Rows of ripening Westport Macomber turnips at Noquochoke Orchards in Westport

John K. Robson

CHAPTER EIGHT

The Man with a Plan

oreclosure, restrictions, suburbanization, government, environmental pressures, corporate farming, NAFTA. These terms and their meanings are part of the hard side of farming, each in their own way contributing to the dramatic decline of our once-strong agricultural heritage. Bankruptcy and "for sale" signs have become the price for many who have tried to hold on to their family businesses in a hostile post-modern environment. When one looks at the realities of modern farming, the view is harsh. Is there help for these small businesses to navigate these dangerous waters? The Plymouth County Conservation District is one group that serves the farmer. They created the position of farm planner, which was then funded by the USDA (United States Department of Agriculture), the Executive Office of Environmental Affairs and the Cape Cod Cranberry Growers Association. This unique position is held by Peter J. Bonome.

Peter Bonome on the Rinta bog in West Wareham

John K. Robson

Peter was raised in North Attleboro, which he saw as "the country." From his earliest years, he was deeply connected to the land. His father Tom worked in construction, building sea walls and jetties, then a common practice to help preserve our coastlines. Peter's attachment to land and sea was manifested in his love for home and in his education choices.

Peter graduated from his studies in soils and water at the University of Rhode Island in 1993. His post-grad work brought him into central Massachusetts working for a watershed association. His study and monitoring of rivers and streams sparked his interest in the concept of sustainable living. While testing waters, Peter was looking for the measure and sources of harmful runoff. The relationship between farmland and water quality became ever more clear. He observed wetland cranberry bogs that use techniques in which water is continually recycled for flooding and irrigation to prevent cross and outside contamination. From that point on, his direction changed and protecting farmland became his passion. Since then he has been working with farmers, especially cranberry growers, to help make the most of what they have; to traverse the obstacle course of ever-changing regulations on various government levels and give them an objective viewpoint of their business. The farm plan is his tool.

So what is a *farm plan*? It is a written document that defines the resources and uses of a farm with the goal of maintaining or enhancing it. The plan includes written history, maps, diagrams, a listing of all its physical assets, as well as problems and solutions to those problems. Records of land and water management and treatment practices, as well as wildlife handling are also offered in detail. The plan will also give step-by-step instruction on how a farmer can develop ideas he or she already has to improve the farm.

Who benefits from this and how? "First of all, the farmer," says Peter. "The plan helps them to organize and getting organized is how we get things done. That is the biggest thing I've learned from this job." The plan also acts as an accountability report card between the farmer and the agencies with whom he has contact: USDA, town, state, Department of Environmental Protection. The plan acts as "a voice on paper" to answer questions or address concerns an agency might have about the farm's water use or actual boundaries, for example. Transfer of ownership is also a lot less complicated because the farm's recent history is all in one neat package. The plan need only be updated every five years. As good as it sounds, a farm plan can only work if, as Peter put it, "the farmer shows willingness to change, look at the difficult parts and work with me."

The four-year-old program is very successful. "We're almost too successful," says Peter. "This is a program that works." The fact that this service is free may actually be one of its weak points. The waiting list of future clients is well over 200. A growth-type company would simply hire more planners, but a nonprofit must keep to its allotted resources. Peter sees the growth potential in marketing the program as a model to companies or similar agencies.

On the personal side, Peter has grown to love his home area even more. Working with farmers to help keep and secure land quality has its own reward because these family farms are long-term, integrity-based businesses. Areas like his hometown "are becoming more homogenized with cities," losing their individual identities to uncontrolled growth. Peter's dedication is rooted in his desire to not only protect, but to assist in the growth and strengthening of agriculture. He attributes the success of the farm plans and the solid reputation of Plymouth County Conservation District as the strongest in the state, to the members of the Cape Cod Cranberry Growers Association. In his relationship with the Association, he has seen the power of a cooperative effort, "moving with one mind," to make changes and proceed ahead.

Index

Bibliography

Araujo, Darlene. "Macomber Turnip Report," Coastal Growers Association, Westport, MA, 1991.

Breed, Donald. "The Turnip That Turned Up in Westport," *Providence Journal Bulletin*, Providence, 1992

Carey, Ann T. and Frederick V. Gifun. *Land Use in Dartmouth, Historical Trends and Present Options*. Southeastern Massachusetts University, 1976.

Comisky, Kathleen Ryan. *Secrets of Old Dartmouth*. New Bedford: Reynolds-DeWalt Printing, Inc., 1976.

Daniels, Jane. "Corn–What to Look For," *Gourmet*, August, 1997.

Drowns, Glenn. "A World of Squash Beyond Zucchini," *Fine Gardening*, September/October, 1988.

Finkel, Harvey, et al. *Wines of New England, A Travel Guide and Tasting Diary*. Brattleboro, VT, 1990.

Goldberg, Howard G. "This Rooster's Got Plenty to Crow About!" *Vineyard & Winery*, September/October, 1997.

Healy, Jonathan L. *The Green Book, Sixth Edition*. Boston: Massachusetts Department of Food and Agriculture, undated.

Hinkle, Richard Paul. "Ripeness vs. Maturity," *Grape Grower*, September, 1991.

Hopley, Claire. "Perfect Partners for Pumpkins," *The Boston Globe*, October, 1991.

Hurd, D. Hamilton. *History of Bristol County Massachusetts with Illustrations*. Philadelphia: J. Lewis & Co., 1883.

Jefferson and Wine. The Plains, VA: Vinifera Wine Growers Association, 1976.

Kummer, C. "Door Stops for Dinner," *Atlantic*, October, 1991.

Lee, Hilde Gabriel. *Serve with Champagne*. Berkeley: Ten Speed Press, 1988.

Lincoln, Joseph C. *Cape Cod Yesterdays*. Boston: Little Brown and Co., 1935.

McCormack, David. *The World of Wine*. New York: Crescent Books, 1986.

McNutt, Joni G. *In Praise of Wine*. Santa Barbara: Capra Press, 1993.

Nathan, Amy. *Fruit*. San Francisco: Chronicle Books, 1988.

Resident and Business Directory, Dartmouth, Westport, Acushnet. Hopkinton, MA: A. E. Foss & Co., 1905.

Root, Waverly and Richard de Rochemont. *Eating in America, A History*. New York: William Morrow and Co., 1976.

Schultz, Christine. "Harvest in Little Compton," *Yankee Magazine*, November, 1997.

Scott, Debra. "Roots: Rediscovering the Wintry Pleasures of Turnips and Parsnips," *Boston Magazine,* September, 1988.

Smith, Susan. "The Legacy of Noquochoke Orchards: Saga of Grandpa George," *Westport Sun*, Summer, 1996.

The Buying Guide for Fresh Fruits, Vegetables, Herbs and Nuts, Eighth Edition. Blue Goose Growers, Inc., 1986.

Thomas, Joseph D. *Cranberry Harvest: A History of Cranberry Growing in Massachusetts*. New Bedford: Spinner Publications, Inc., 1990.

Town of Dartmouth Viticultural Feasibility Study. February, 1997.

Travers, Milton. *One of the Keys, The Wampanoag Indian Contribution*. Dartmouth Massachusetts Bicentennial Commission. The Christopher Publishing House, 1975.

Viereck, Philip. *The New Land: Discovery, Exploration, and Early Settlement of Northeastern United States from Earliest Voyages to 1621, Told in the Words of the Explorers Themselves*. New York: The John Day Co., 1967.

Webster's New Encyclopedic Dictionary. New York: Black Dog and Leventhal Publishers, 1993.